W9-BRS-538

Contents

CONTENTS

3

Introducing Prague

Two decades after the Velvet Revolution, Prague is the short-break destination of choice for millions of visitors. Its rich culture and a miraculously preserved architectural heritage more than meet their expectations.

Built on both banks of the Vltava and with a castle atop a rocky spur, Prague is a glorious fusion of nature and architecture. It is the very image of what a capital city was before the onset of the industrial age. Woods and orchards sweep down to the water's edge, while the skyline is pierced by myriad towers and steeples. Buildings of every era stand side by side, from burgher's house to baroque palace, from art nouveau apartment block to Cubist café. The historic hub is compact enough to be easily explored on foot (though the excellent public transport system can help take the strain).

In the 1990s, when the world started to come to a Prague that it had ignored for so long, many locals felt excluded, resentful that the city had been taken over by foreigners. Times have changed; while tourism has become a mainstay of the economy, increasingly prosperous Czechs have begun to reclaim their territory. Sleek modern hotels and daring fusion restaurants are no longer just the preserve of visitors, and bars and cafés are filled with stylishly attired young locals.

Prague's guests are better catered to than ever before; as well as an expanding choice of places to sleep and eat, once-dusty museums are modernizing, and glittering new attractions include a museum for the city's most famous literary son, Franz Kafka. Beware of Prague's embrace! It was Kafka who warned of Prague that 'this little mother has claws', and once in her grasp you may find it difficult to leave.

Facts + Figures

- Prague's population is 1.15 million.
- Czechs drink an average of 160 litres (338 pints) of beer per person per year.
- The city has 10,000 works of art and protected objects.

THE 1,000-YEAR FLOOD

The usually tranquil Vltava can present another, fiercer face, as in 1890, when its waters rose and swept away three arches of Charles Bridge. But the worst-ever flood came in August 2002, when whole districts were under water, thousands of people had to be evacuated and billions of crowns of damage were caused.

PRAGUE PEOPLE

Half of Prague's 1,150,000 citizens live in *paneláks*, the high-rise, prefabricated apartment blocks of Communist times that form a ring around the city. Those who can afford it are opting to move to the greener surroundings and fresher air in the countryside beyond, creating a commuting culture that hardly existed before.

VISITORS TO THE RESCUE

Even before Communism, Prague was an important manufacturing base, and the totalitarian regime promoted industries of all kinds. Since 1989 tourism has taken over from industry as the city's big earner, helping to keep unemployment at virtually nil and income levels much higher than in the rest of the country.

A Short Stay in Prague

DAY 1

Morning Start on the steps in front of the **Národní Muzeum** (▷ 48) with a view down Václavské náměstí. Go through the underpass to the statue of Good King Wenceslas, then walk down the square. Look into the Lucerna Passage and admire mischievous artist David Černý's zany take on the Wenceslas statue. At the foot of the square head west along 28 října and Národní třída to catch the No. 22 (Bílá Hora) or 23 (Malovanka) tram from the stop behind the Tesco store. Enjoy the ride across the **River Vltava** (▷ 52), through Malá Strana and up to Pražský hrad. Linger in the courtyards, looking into the Old Royal Palace, **Katedrála sv Víta** (▷ 68) and Golden Lane. Descend to Malá Strana via steep **Nerudova** (▷ 89), marvel at the baroque interior of **Chrám sv Mikuláše** (▷ 84), then go through the lanes to tranquil Kampa Island.

Lunch Enjoy lunch in the riverside restaurant attached to the **Muzeum Kampa** (▷ 89).

Afternoon Cross the Vltava via **Karlův most** (▷ 28) and lose yourself among the labyrinthine lanes of the Old Town before finding your way to **Staroměstské náměstí** (▷ 32), making sure that you are there on the hour to see the Astronomical Clock in action.

Dinner Tuck into a substantial Czech feast of duck, cabbage and dumplings at one of the Kolkovna group's superpubs, for example **Kolkovna** (▷ 41).

Evening Continue your night out in one of the city's traditional pubs such as **U Fleků** (▷ 62) or **U Medvídků** (▷ 42).

DAY 2

Morning Board tram 22 or 23 at a convenient point and ride to the Pohořelec stop. Admire the halls of **Strahovský klášter** (▷ 74) then soak up the glorious city panorama. Catch the carillon at the **Loreta** (▷ 70) and time your arrival at the western entrance of the castle to watch the midday changing of the guard. Go down to Malá Strana via Nové zámecké schody (New Castle Steps) and walk through **Valdštejnský palác** (▷ 88) and its garden to the little riverside park at the end of Mánes Bridge, from where you can pause for a break and take in the an unusual view across the river to Charles Bridge and the Old Town.

Lunch Enjoy a meal at the **Hergetova cihelna** restaurant (▷ 94).

Afternoon Retrace your steps to Malostranská station and travel two stops to Můstek. On emerging from the station, walk northeastwards along Na Příkopě, one of the city's foremost shopping streets, to the **Prašná brána/Powder Tower** (▷ 36) and the **Obecní dům/Municipal House** (▷ 30). After a conducted tour of the fabulous art nouveau interiors of the Municipal House, relax with coffee and cakes in its sumptuous café. Afterward, go a short distance along Celetná, admiring the Black Madonna building before turning right through a passageway to Štupártská and Malá Štupartská, then beneath the archway into Týn Court. Cross Old Town Square to the Pařížská shopping boulevard and **Josefov** (▷ 26), visiting the Old/New Synagogue and the Old Jewish Cemetery.

Dinner Dine at a restaurant with a view—**Petřínské terasy** (▷ 94).

Evening Be thrilled by opera or ballet in the **Národní divadlo** (▷ 60).

This is a quick guide to the Top 25, which are described in more detail later. Here they are listed alphabetically, and the tinted background shows the area they are in.

Zoologická zahrada
Trojský zámek
zámecká zahrada
TROJA
Vltava

BUBENEČ
Stromovka

HOLEŠOVICE

Veletržní palác

LETNÁ
Národní technické muzeum
Letenské sady
Ostrov Štvanice

HRADČANY
63–80
Králivská zahrada
HRADČANY Katedrála sv Víta
Šternberský palác
Bazilika a klášter sv Jiří
Palácové zahrady
Pražský hrad
Valdštejnský palác
Loreta
Chrám sv Mikuláše
Malostranské náměstí
Strahovský klášter
Lobkovická zahrada
Strahovská zahrada
MALÁ STRANA
Semínářská zahrada
KAMPA
STRAHOV
Petřín
Petřínské sady
Střelecký ostrov
Národní divadlo
MALÁ STRANA
81–94
Kinského zahrada
Dětský ostrov
Slovanský ostrov

STARÉ MĚSTO
21–42
Anežský klášter
Uměleckoprůmyslové muzeum
JOSEFOV STARÉ MĚSTO
Obecní dům
Staroměstské náměstí
Muchovo muzeum
Václavské náměstí
Riegrovy sady
Národní muzeum

NOVÉ MĚSTO

Husovy sady

SMÍCHOV
Santoška

NOVÉ MĚSTO
43–62
VYŠEHRAD
Vyšehradské sady

Malvazinky
Císařská louka

9

Shopping

It's increasingly hard for visitors to escape uniformity and find local products worth taking home. Thanks to their long tradition as craftspeople and artisans, however, the Czechs have plenty to offer. Along with crystal and garnets, don't overlook the herbal liqueur Becherovka, blue onion porcelain and art books.

Antiques
Antiques stores, found under signs reading *starožítnictví*, *bazar* or *vetešnictví* (junk shop), contain many treasures: Quality paintings, kitchenware, jewellery and linens can be found at reasonable prices. Many bazaars specialize in old cameras, clocks and other mechanical devices.

Fashion
A number of Czech fashion designers are making a name for themselves and have opened successful boutiques where you can find original pieces at a fraction of what you'd pay at home for a similar-quality item. Most of these shops are concentrated on a few streets north of Old Town Square—Dlouhá, Dušní and V Kolkovně. Fashionable international names line nearby Pařížska, but don't expect bargains there.

Books
Considering the Czechs' contribution to art, architecture and photography, it's not

From antique books to toys and painted eggs to glass, Prague has plenty of good souvenir choices

---

SPA TREATS

A whole culture has grown up around Czech spa towns. Re-create this atmosphere at home by strolling about, sipping water from a porcelain cup with a built-in straw and sipping spa waters, or *oplátky*. The cups can be found cheaply in antiques shops. Round off your cure with a shot of Becherovka, the herbal liqueur developed by a spa doctor in Karlovy Vary in 1807. It's said to be especially good for stomach ailments.

surprising that handsome coffee-table books devoted to subjects such as Czech cubism, avant-garde photography and the art nouveau movement are popular.

Glassware

Glass and crystal, of course, are ubiquitous, and the sheer number of shops and variety of products can be overwhelming. But Czech crystal is famous for a reason and should not be overlooked. Stick to shops affiliated with just one or two manufacturers that focus primarily on tableware and larger individual pieces and you're likely to take home something of real quality. Look for hand-blown, hand-cut lead crystal produced by names such as Moser and Sklo Bohemia, and Desná for art deco.

Souvenirs

Much of what is sold in the tourist areas has no relation to local traditions or culture: Russian dolls, Polish amber and non-Czech crystal. Lace tablecloths are more likely to have been made in Russian factories. If any of these products catches your eye and doesn't break the bank there's nothing wrong in buying it—but if your heart is set on a real Czech souvenir, keep looking.

NOT ALL GARNETS ARE CREATED EQUAL

The Czechs have been mining garnets for centuries. Said to bring vitality and cure depression, the Bohemian variety of garnet is not found anywhere else in the world. They are a deep, rich red known as 'dove's blood' and the settings typically feature many small garnets clustered together. Most garnet jewellery is made by the cooperative Granát Turnov and sold in factory stores and by authorized dealers with a stamp of approval. However, a fair amount of what is sold in Prague as Bohemian garnets is actually made from almandines or other stones from Italy and elsewhere. Showy gold pieces set with large, brownish stones are not Bohemian garnets.

Shopping by Theme

Whether you're looking for a department store, a quirky boutique, or something in between, you'll find it all in Prague. On this page shops are listed by theme. For a more detailed write-up, see the individual listings in Prague by Area.

ANTIQUES

Ahasver Antiques (▷ 92)
Alma Antique (▷ 38)
Dorotheum (▷ 39)
Hodinářství Václav Matouš (▷ 57)
Modernista (▷ 39)

ARTS AND CRAFTS

Galerie Peithner-Lichtenfels (▷ 39)

BOOKS

Academia (▷ 57)
Anagram (▷ 38)
Antikvariát Gallerie Můstek(▷ 57)
Antikvariát Karel Krenek (▷ 38)
Antikvariát Pařížská (▷ 38)
Big Ben Bookshop (▷ 38)
Gambra (▷ 79)
Globe Bookstore and Coffeehouse (▷ 57)
Hatle Antikvariát (▷ 57)
Kiwi (▷ 57)
Kožešiny Kubín (▷ 92)
Palác Knih Luxor (▷ 58)
U Zlaté Číše (▷ 92)

COSMETICS

Botanicus (▷ 38)

FASHION

Boheme (▷ 38)
Elazar (▷ 57)
Myslivost (▷ 58)
Pavla A Olga (▷ 92)
Timoure et Group (▷ 39)

FOOD AND WINE

Cellarius (▷ 57)
Country Life (▷ 38)
Culinaria (▷ 38)
Havelský trh (▷ 39)
Vino Ungelt (▷ 39)

GLASS AND CERAMICS

Art Deco (▷ 38)
Artěl (▷ 38)
Celetná Crystal (▷ 38)
Dům Porcelánu (▷ 57)
Moser (▷ 58)

HANDICRAFTS AND SOUVENIRS

Manufaktura (▷ 39)
Museum Shop (▷ 79)
Original Souvenir (▷ 58)
Qubus (▷ 39)
Zlatá Ulička (▷ 79)

JEWELLERY

Granát (▷ 39)

MUSIC

Agharta (▷ 38)
Bontonland (▷ 57)
Kliment (▷ 58)

PHOTOGRAPHY

Centrum Fotoškoda (▷ 57)

STORES

Kotva (▷ 39)
Lucerna Passage (▷ 58)
Palladium (▷ 58)
Slovanský dům (▷ 58)
Tesco (▷ 58)

TOYS AND GAMES

Hřacký (▷ 79)
Obchod S Loutkami (▷ 92)

Prague by Night

Drinking in Prague

Prague has no shortage of hip dance clubs and trendy bars, but for most Czechs, the best nights are spent in a pub. No visitor should pass up the opportunity to taste an expertly poured Pilsner or Budvar at the long wooden tables of a typical Czech pub. An alternative is the *vinárna* (wine bar). A *vinárna* can be a restaurant, but more typically is a small establishment, sometimes with standing room only, offering inexpensive Czech wines, often of surprisingly good quality.

All That Jazz

Czechs are known for being a musical nation and on any given night there are a variety of concerts on offer, from local modern jazz fixtures like Emil Viklický to touring Balkan gypsy bands to performances of Dvořák and Smetana. Postage-stamp jazz joints abound in downtown and larger venues like Roxy (▷ 40) and Palác Akropolis (▷ 60) book an eclectic mix of acts.

Staying Out Late

Night owls thirsty for a cocktail should head for the bars just north of Old Town Square. Another district that's home to hip bars and clubs is along Karoliny světlé near the embankment south of Old Town. Of course you can always take a romantic stroll and view the floodlit castle from the blissfully empty Charles Bridge.

There are a variety of nighttime activities: traditional dancing, classical music, clubs and pubs

---

WHAT'S ON

The best source of information for English-language readers about what's on in Prague is probably the tabloid 'Night and Day' section of the weekly newspaper *Prague Post.*
Tickets for events can be obtained at box offices (which may be less expensive) or through Ticketpro (☎ 234 704 234; www.ticketpro.cz) or Bohemia Ticket (☎ 224 227 832; www.bohemiaticket.cz).

Eating Out

Traditional Czech food is similar to other central European regional cuisines. Most dishes are built around pork, with the national dish being roast pork, served with thinly sliced bread dumplings and a sweetish sauerkraut—known to locals as *vepřo, knedlo* or *zelo*.

More preferences
Particularly popular is goulash—*gulář*. Another dish to look for is *svíčková*—a strip of beef tenderloin, served in gravy and topped with cranberry relish and a lemon. You'll also usually find very good roast duck or veal. Desserts are a high point. The best place to find Czech food is at a traditional pub, where you can wash it down with a glass of some of the world's best beer.

International and Fast-Food Dining
Prague is filled with restaurants from all around the world and the quality is rising every year. Unfortunately, Prague is no longer considered a cheap place to eat. As for fast food, McDonald's, KFC and Starbucks are all here, along with the local competitors.

Drinks
Czechs are world famous for the quality of their beer. Light lagers are still far and away the most common, but increasingly brewers are adding dark beers to their lineups. The most popular spirits include the ever-present *slivovice*, a high-octane plum brandy.

WHERE TO DINE
With a wide choice of places to eat, it's worthwhile choosing somewhere with a distinctive setting, of which there are many. You can dine in the stately ambience of an historic palace, sit at a table with a stunning view over spires and rooftops or the swiftly flowing Vltava, or enjoy a hearty repast beneath the vaults of a medieval cellar.

From grand old eateries to modern-day sandwich outlets you will find a good range of cuisine

Restaurants by Cuisine

There are restaurants to suit all tastes and budgets in Prague. On this page they are listed by cuisine. For a more detailed description of each restaurant, see Prague by Area.

If You Like...

However you'd like to spend your time in Prague, these top suggestions should help you tailor your ideal visit. Each sight or listing has a fuller write-up elsewhere in the book.

UNUSUAL ANTIQUES

Enhance your appreciation of Bohemian glass and porcelain by studying the stunning exhibits at the Uměleckoprůmyslové muzeum (UPM – Applied Arts Museum, ▷ 34).
Avoid the souvenir shops along the tourist trail, and look instead at the Dorotheum (▷ 39).
Bargain at reputable antiques establishments such as Alma Antique (▷ 38).

Glassware and antiques are worth seeking out in Prague

HISTORIC HOTELS

Look for luxurious lodgings behind the baroque façade of the Hotel Aria (▷ 112) in Malá Strana.
Take up residence in the Mandarin Oriental Hotel (▷ 112), an exquisitely sensitive conversion of a 14th-century monastery in the quietest part of Malá Strana.
Luxuriate in the stylish K&K Central Hotel (▷ 112), a jewel of art nouveau architecture and interior design.

DINING WITH A VIEW

Dine with a table-side view of Prague Castle at Bellevue (▷ 41).
Take the elevator to the top of Frank Gehry's 'Dancing Building' overlooking the Vltava, and enjoy the French cuisine of La Perle de Prague (▷ 62).
Enjoy countrified views from Petřínské terasy, perched amid the greenery of Petřín Hill (▷ 94).
Gaze down over Malá Strana from U zlaté studně (▷ 80), tucked away against the Castle ramparts.

Try local fare to get a true taste of the city

CZECH COOKING

Tuck into traditional Czech food pre-pared as if it were haute cuisine at Černý Kohout (▷ 61).

Sate your appetite with hearty Bohemian fare at U Pinkasů (▷ 62), and wash it down with well-kept Pilsner Urquell.

Enjoy duck and dumplings at Kolkovna (▷ 41), a refined version of the classic Czech pub.

BEING PAMPERED

Relax in the wellness area of a five-star hotel (some of which are open to nonguests), none of which outclasses the superb spa that is part of the Mandarin Oriental Hotel (▷ 112).

Find your way to the Sabai Studio in the Slovanský dům arcade, and submit to the attentions of qualified massage therapists, whose treatments have been developed in Thailand for more than a thousand years.

GREAT JAZZ

Find your own way to relax—at a spa or enjoying a massage

Force your way into the cramped basement of U malého Glena (▷ 92) to soak up some of the city's best jazz.

Descend into a Gothic cellar at AghaRTA Jazz Centrum (▷ 40) for an evening you won't

forget, with some of the top names in jazz performing regularly.

Ignore the misleading name (The Old Lady), hot sessions are a nightly rule at Jazz Club U staré paní (▷ 40).

Live music—be it jazz, traditional or contemporary can be enjoyed in a variety of venues

KEEPING THE KIDS HAPPY

There are activities to involve your children

Take them up to the top of Petřín Hill in the funicular and watch them split their sides at the distorting mirrors of the Bludiště (▷ 87).

Exploring the city by tram can be exciting for kids used to being ferried around in cars. Bear in mind that you get the best views by standing right at the back.

Visit the Výstaviště Praha (▷ 104), whose attractions include a funfair and a local version of Sea World called Mořský svět, then continue out of town to the Zoo.

GETTING UP HIGH

Brave the high-speed elevator of the Televizní vysílač/TV Tower in Žižkov for a view extending over 100km (62 miles).

Toil up the endless steps of the tower of Chrám sv Mikuláše (▷ 84) and emerge high above the red rooftops of Malá Strana.

Climb toward heaven via the winding staircase of the south tower of Katedrála sv Víta (▷ 68) for a panorama otherwise enjoyed only by angels.

SEEING THE CITY IN STYLE

Take to the water for a pleasure cruise along the Vltava (▷ 52).

Hop aboard a vintage tram (▷ 119) for a nostalgic trip along the tracks.

Sit in a stylish Škoda or other old-timer and be driven round the sights.

Take to the waters to see the city from the Vltava River. Boat trips head downstream and most pass under five bridges. In fine weather you can opt to sit outside as you view the city from a different angle

Prague by Area

STARÉ MĚSTO

NOVÉ MĚSTO

HRADČANY

MALÁ STRANA

FARTHER AFIELD

Within the Old Town's labyrinth of lanes is the greatest concentration of Prague's historic buildings, plus intriguing shops, bars and restaurants. Close by is Josefov, the historic Jewish quarter.

Čechův most

náměstí Curieových

Dvořákovo

sv Šimon a Juda

Dušní

Kozí

Právnická fakulta

Dvořákovo nábřeží

U milosrdných

El Krásnohorské

Pařížská

Bílkova

Kozí

UK

Břehová

ČVUT
Konzerv

17 listopadu

Na rejdišti

U st. školy

Vězeňská

Umĕleckoprůmyslové muzeum

Dušní

V Kolkovně

Bitova

Kozí

Rudolfinum

Pařížská

Staronová Synagóga

Mánesův most

Široká

Maiselova

Dlouhá

Alšovo nábřeží

JOSEFOV

Kaprova

Jáchymova

Žatecká

Palác Kinských

Staroměstská

Valentinská

Veleslavin

Exposice
Franze Kafky

Křižovnická

Staroměstské náměstí

Platnéřská

Pařížská

Kostel Panny
Marie Před Týnem

Železná

Mariánské náměstí

Husova

Staroměstská radnice

Karlův most

Karlův most

Křižovnické náměstí

Klementinum

Malé náměstí

Melantrichova

Kožná

Kaprova

Muzeum
loutkářských
kultur

Kariova

Dům pánu z Kunštátu
a Podebrad

sv Havel

Muzeum
Bedřicha
Smetany

nábřeží

Liliová

Řetězová

Michalská

Haveiská

Anenska

sv Jilji

Karlovy
lázně

Smetanovo nábřeží

Stříbrná

Náprstkova

Betlémská
kaple

Husova

Jilská

Vejvodova

V Kotcích

Rytířská

Skořepka

Perlová

V l t a v a

0   250 m

0   250 yds

Anežský klášter

HIGHLIGHTS

● *Madonna of Vyšehrad* painting
● *Madonna and Child* sculpture from Český Krumlov
● Panel paintings by the Master of Vyšší Brod
● Portraits of saints by Master Theodoricus
● *Christ on the Mount of Olives* by the Třeboň Master
● Votive altarpiece from Zlíchov
● *Madonna of Poleň*, Cranach the Elder
● Vaulted medieval cloister
● Church of St. Francis (concert hall)
● Church of the Holy Saviour

St. Agnes's Convent, the city's most venerable Gothic complex, shelters in a quiet precinct of the Old Town. Once earmarked for destruction, it is now the fitting home for one of the country's most distinctive galleries.

Canonized Czech Agnes was a 13th-century princess and founder of a convent of Poor Clares here. In its glory days St. Agnes's was a mausoleum for the royal family, but was it sacked by the Hussites in the 15th century. In 1782, it was closed down by Joseph II, and became slum housing until city authorities decided to raze it in the 1890s, only relenting when faced with bitter public protest. The convent was slowly restored, and, in November 1989, days before the Communist

Church of Sv František (St. Francis of Assisi) in Anežský klášter (left); the altarpiece called Resurrection *by the Master of the Trebon, 1380, in Anežský klášter (middle); Church of Sv Salvator (Holy Saviour, below)*

regime ended, Agnes was made a saint. An auspicious omen?

Medieval masterpieces The convent now displays the National Gallery's collection of medieval art from Czech lands and nearby. The magnificent works show the extraordinary achievements in the fine arts in Bohemia, above all during the reigns of Emperor Charles IV and his successors. Prague's court artists fused Italian, French and Flemish influences in a manner all their own, pointing toward the late-Gothic style that flourished in Europe.

Look down The vista to St. Agnes's Convent from Letná Plain on the far side of the Vltava gives a fascinating overview of this medieval riverside complex of buildings.

THE BASICS

www.ngprague.cz
➕ G6
✉ U Milosrdných 17
☎ 221 879 216; 224 810 628
🕐 Tue–Sun 10–6
Ⓜ Náměstí Republiky
🚋 Tram 17 (Právnická fakulta stop) or tram 5, 8, 14 (Dlouhá třída stop)
♿ Fair
💰 Moderate

Josefov

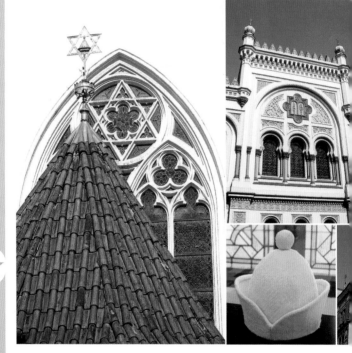

HIGHLIGHTS

● Vine carving in entrance portal
● Tombstone of Rabbi Loew (1525–1609)

TIP

● Remember that the Old/New Synagogue is still a place of worship for the Jewish community, and that men should cover their heads, both here and in the cemetery (paper *kippah* are available).

With its synagogues and age-old cemetery, Josefov is one of the most evocative sites of Jewish heritage anywhere, testimony to a world that lasted for a thousand years until brought to an end by the brutal Nazi occupation.

Ghetto memories Josefov owes its name to the liberal Emperor Josef II, who emancipated the Jews in 1781, but the ghetto itself dates from the 13th century, when its high walls kept its inhabitants in and the Christian residents out. Over time it produced many remarkable characters, foremost among them, learned Rabbi Loew, creator of that archetypal man-made monster, the Golem. The ghetto's warren of twisting lanes and dark courtyards was swept away in an effort to clean up the city in the late

Clockwise from left: Maiselova Synagoga; Španělská Synagoga or Spanish Synagogue; view along Kaprova Street; art nouveau detail on Kaprova street; statue of a walking headless figure with Franz Kafka; art nouveau apartments; the emblem of the Prague Jewish Community (replica) in the Maiselova Synagoga

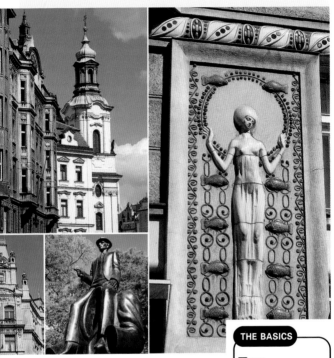

19th century, when only its synagogues, cemetery and rococo Town Hall were spared. During World War II, the Nazis deported nearly all of Prague's Jews to the prison town of Terezín and then to Auschwitz. Some of the valuables they stole from Jewish communities are now on display in the synagogues.

The Old/New Synagogue With its pointed brick gable and atmospheric interior, the Gothic synagogue of 1275 is the oldest functioning in Europe, a compelling reminder of the age-old intertwining of Jewish and Christian cultures.

Old Jewish Cemetery The total number laid to rest beneath the dappled shade of the tall trees may amount to 12,000, laid on top of one another, up to 12 deep in places.

THE BASICS

✚ F6/7
✉ Cemetery: enter through Pinkas Synagogue Široka 3
☎ Prague Jewish Museum: 224 317 191; www.jewishmuseum.cz
🕐 Jewish Museum: Apr–Oct Sun–Fri 9–6; rest of year 9–4.30. Closed Jewish holidays. Old/New Synagogue: Sun–Thu 9.30–5, Fri 9–4
🚇 Staroměstska
♿ Fair
💷 Cemetery/museums: expensive. Old/New Synagogue: moderate

Karlův most

TOP 25

● Old Town Bridge Tower
● Malá Strana Bridge Tower (viewpoint)
● Nepomuk statue with bronze relief panels
● Bruncvík (Roland column) to southwest
● Statue of St. John of Matha
● Bronze crucifix with Hebrew inscription
● Statue of St. Luitgard (by Braun)

TIP

● To experience a non-crowded Charles Bridge you need to get there early in the morning, even out of season.

Any time is right to visit Charles Bridge, the magnificent medieval crossing over the Vltava. Enjoy the hucksters, then enjoy the almost sinister dusk, when sculpted saints on the parapets gesticulate against the darkening sky.

Gothic overpass For centuries Karlův most was Prague's only bridge, built on the orders of Emperor Charles IV in the 14th century. It's a triumph of Gothic engineering, with 16 massive sandstone arches carrying it more than 490m (534 yards) from the Old Town to soar across the Vltava River and Kampa Island to touch down near the heart of Malá Strana. It is protected by sturdy timber cutwaters and guarded at both ends by towers; the eastern face of the Old Town Bridge Tower is richly ornamented.

Clockwise from left: people passing artists and vendors on Charles Bridge; statues line the bridge; the Castle with the bridge in front; detail of the clock tower of the Naprstek Museum, seen from the bridge; St. John Nepomuk (patron saint of bridges) with his five-star halo; looking along the bridge

Its opposite number has a smaller tower, once part of the earlier Judith Bridge.

Starry saint Charles Bridge has always been much more than a river crossing. Today's traders succeed earlier merchants and stall-holders, and tournaments, battles and executions have all been held on the bridge. The heads of the Protestants executed in 1621 in Old Town Square were displayed here. Later that century the bridge was beautified with baroque sculptures, including the statue of St. John Nepomuk. Falling foul of the king, this unfortunate cleric was pushed off the bridge in a sack. As his body bobbed in the water, five stars danced on the surface. Nepomuk hence became the patron saint of bridges, and is always depicted with his starry halo.

THE BASICS

➕ E7
✉ Staroměstská
🚋 Tram 12, 22, 23 to Malostranské náměstí
♿ Good
💷 Bridge free

Obecní dům

Exterior and interior views of the Municipal House

THE BASICS

🔲 G7
✉ Náměstí Republiky 5
☎ 222 002 121
⏱ Check locally
🚇 Náměstí Republiky
♿ Few

HIGHLIGHTS

● Entrance canopy and mosaic *Homage to Prague*
● Smetanova síň (Smetana Hall), with frescoes symbolizing the dramatic arts
● Mayor's Suite, with paintings by Mucha
● Rieger Hall, with Myslbek sculptures
● Palacký Room, with paintings by Preisler

The prosaic name 'Municipal House' fails utterly to convey anything of the character of this extraordinary art nouveau building, a gloriously extravagant early-20th-century confection on which every artist of the day seems to have left his stamp.

City council citadel Glittering like some gigantic, flamboyant jewel, more brightly than ever since its 1997 restoration, the Obecní dům is linked to the blackened Prašná brána (Powder Tower, ▷ 36), last relic of the Old Town's fortifications and long one of the city's main symbols. The intention of the city fathers in the first years of the 20th century was to add an even more powerful element to the cityscape that would celebrate the glory of the Czech nation and Prague's place within it. The site of the old Royal Palace was selected, and no expense was spared to erect a megastructure in which the city's burgeoning life could expand. Begun in 1902, the great edifice was ceremonially opened in 1911.

Ornamental orgy The building schedule included meeting and assembly rooms, cafés, restaurants, bars, even a pâtisserie, while the mayor was provided with particularly luxurious quarters. The 1,149-seat Smetana Hall, home of the Prague Symphony Orchestra, is a temple to the muse of Bohemian music. Everything is encrusted with lavish decoration, in stucco, glass, mosaic, murals, metalwork and textiles.

Staroměstské náměstí

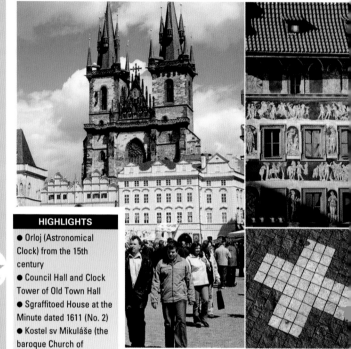

HIGHLIGHTS

● Orloj (Astronomical Clock) from the 15th century
● Council Hall and Clock Tower of Old Town Hall
● Sgraffitoed House at the Minute dated 1611 (No. 2)
● Kostel sv Mikuláše (the baroque Church of St. Nicholas)
● Jan Hus Memorial of 1915
● Palác Kinských (▷ 36)
● The Gothic Dům u Kamenného Zvonu (House at the Stone Bell)
● Arcaded houses Nos. 22–26, with baroque façades and medieval interiors and cellars

TIP

● Climb the tower of the Old Town Hall for one of the best views over Prague's red-tiled roofs.

Visitors throng the Old Town Square all year, entertained by street performers, refreshed at outdoor cafés and enchanted by the Astronomical Clock and the cheerful façades of the old buildings.

Martyrs and mournful memories The Old Town Square has not always been so jolly. The marketplace became a scene of execution of Hussites in the 15th century and 27 prominent Protestants were put to death in 1621 (they are commemorated by white crosses in the paving stones). In 1945, in a final act of spite, diehard Nazis demolished a whole wing of the Old Town Hall; the site has still not been built on.

Striking clock First installed during the 15th century, the Orloj (Astronomical Clock) shows

Clockwise from the left: Old Town Square with Týn Church in the background; detail of a decorated house of 1610; the Astronomical Clock; the square in the sunshine; the painted calendar below the Astronomical Clock; one of the 27 white crosses which are set in the paving stones before the chapel

the position of the sun, moon and stars, while its lower dial shows the signs of the Zodiac and the changes of the seasons. Its hourly procession of carved figures is one of the city's great spectacles.

Around the square The hub of the square is the Jan Hus Memorial, an extraordinary art nouveau sculpture whose base is one of the few places in the square where you can sit without having to buy a drink. To one side rise the blackened towers of the Týn Church (▷ 36), while to the other is the Old Town Hall, an attractively varied assembly of buildings and, a bit farther, the city's second St. Nicholas's Church. The fine town houses surrounding the square are a study in various architectural styles from Gothic to baroque, rococo, and finally Gothic Revival.

THE BASICS

➕ F7

✉ Staroměstské náměstí

🍴 Restaurants and cafés

Ⓜ Staroměstská

♿ Fair

Uměleckoprůmyslové muzeum

The exterior of the museum (middle); stained glass (left); an exhibit (below)

THE BASICS

www.upm.cz

F6

17 listopadu 2

251 093 111

Tue 10–7, Wed–Sun 10–6

Café Mon–Fri 10–6; Sat, Sun 10.30–6

Staroměstská

Few

Moderate

HIGHLIGHTS

● Pietra dura scene of a town by Castnicci
● Beer glasses engraved with card players
● Boulle commode and cabinet
● Monumental baroque furniture by Dientzenhofer and Santini
● Meissen Turk on a rhino
● Holic porcelain figures
● Harrachov glass
● Klášterec figurines of Prague characters
● Biedermeier cradle
● Surprise view down into the Old Jewish Cemetery

The pompous façade of Prague's Decorative Arts Museum merely hints at the riches within. A steep flight of stairs leads visitors to treasure chambers full of fine furniture, glass, porcelain, clocks and more.

Riverside reclaimed Looking something like a miniature Louvre, the Decorative Arts Museum was built in 1901 in an area that, by the end of the 19th century, had turned its back on the river and become a jumble of storage depots and timber yards. The city leaders decided to beautify it with fine public buildings and riverside promenades. The School of Arts and Crafts (1884) and the Rudolfinum concert hall and gallery (1890) preceded the museum; the University's Philosophy Building (1929), which completed the enclosure of what is now Jan Palach Square, followed it.

Decorative delights The museum's collections are incredibly rich and diverse, numbering nearly 200,000 objects from all over the world, but with special emphasis on the glorious craft heritage of the Czech lands. Carefully chosen items are arranged in a series of imaginative themed displays such as 'Story of the Fribe' (covering textiles of all kinds), 'Born in Fire' (glass and porcelain) and 'Print and Image' (books, graphics and photography). While there are objects from every era, the contribution on the art nouveau and art deco movements are particularly rich.

More to See

BETLÉMSKÁ KAPLE (BETHLEHEM CHAPEL)

You must see this barnlike structure where Jan Hus preached to really appreciate the deeply nonconformist traditions so thoroughly obscured by centuries of imposed Catholicism. The chapel, in the Old Town, was totally reconstructed in the 1950s.

➕ F7 ✉ Betlémské náměstí 🕐 Apr–end Oct Tue–Sun 10–6.30; Nov–end Mar 10–5.30 🍴 Restaurants and cafés nearby 🚇 Národní třída 💰 Inexpensive

DŮM U ČERNÉ MATKY BOŽÍ (HOUSE AT THE BLACK MADONNA)

This striking example of Czech Cubist architecture, designed by Josef Gočár (1912), stands squarely at the corner of Celetná Street in the heart of the Old Town. It houses a fine collection of Czech Cubism.

➕ G7 ✉ Ovocný trh 19 ☎ 224 211 746 🕐 Daily Tue–Sun 10–6 🚇 Náměstí Republiky 💰 Moderate

DŮM U ZLATÉHO PRSTENU (HOUSE AT THE GOLDEN RING)

The Prague City Gallery's fine collection of 20th- and 21st-century Czech art is housed here. The gallery stages large exhibitions a few steps away at the House at the Stone Bell, a Gothic tower house that restorers discovered behind a rococo façade in the 1960s.

➕ G7 ✉ Týnská 6 ☎ 224 827 022 🕐 Tue–Sun 10–6 🍴 Cafés and restaurants 🚇 Staroměstská 💰 Moderate

KLEMENTINUM

Now the home of the National Library, this vast complex arranged around a sequence of courtyards was begun by the Jesuits in the late 16th century. A guided tour takes in some of the sumptuous interiors, but only concertgoers get to see the gorgeous Mirror Chapel.

➕ F7 ✉ Klementinum ☎ 221 663 111 🕐 Core hours: daily 2–6 🍴 Cafés and restaurants 🚇 Staroměstská 💰 Moderate

The Black Madonna House is a Cubist style building that houses the museum of Czech Cubism

The baroque Library Hall in the Klementinum

KOSTEL PANNY MARIE PŘED TÝNEM (TÝN CHURCH)

Among the city's best-known land-marks is this Gothic church, whose twin towers stick up spikily behind the houses of Old Town Square. Inside are some fascinating tombs.
➕ G7 ✉ Enter from Staroměstská náměstí under the red address marker 604 🕓 Tue–Sun 10–1, 3–5 🍽 Cafés and restaurants nearby 🚇 Staroměstská

MUZEUM BEDŘICHA SMETANY (SMETANA MUSEUM)

The museum dedicated to the com-poser of 'Vltava' is appropriately in a building that rises out of the river.
➕ E7 ✉ Novotného lávka 1 ☎ 222 220 082 🕓 Wed–Mon 10–12, 1–5 🚇 Staroměstská 💶 Inexpensive

PALÁC KINSKÝCH (KINSKY PALACE)

Franz Kafka once attended school here and his father ran a haberdash-ery shop on the ground floor of this lovely rococo palace. In February 1948 the Communist coup d'etat was proclaimed from its balcony. It's part of the National Gallery, with fine Czech landscape paintings.
➕ F7 ✉ Staroměstské náměstí 12 ☎ 224 810 758 🕓 Tue–Sun 10–6 🚇 Staroměstská 💶 Moderate

PRAŠNÁ BRÁNA (POWDER TOWER)

This famous gateway, with its chisel roof, was built as a ceremo-nial entrance to the Old Town. The climb to the top is worthwhile for the views.
➕ G7 ✉ Celetná 🕓 Apr–early Nov daily 10–6 🚇 Náměstí Republiky 🚊 Trams 5, 14 to Náměstí Republiky 💶 Inexpensive

STAVOVSKÉ DIVADLO (ESTATES THEATRE)

The venue that saw the premiere of Mozart's Don Giovanni in 1787 is a marvel of pristine neoclassical glory. Performances of Wolfgang's great-est hits can be enjoyed here.
➕ G7 ✉ Ovocný trh ☎ 224 901 448 🚇 Můstek

Powder Gate Tower
(Prašná Brána)

The Estates Theatre,
Stavovské divadlo

Staré Město

Explore the crooked streets and squares of the Old Town on a walk that dips in and out of the Royal Way.

DISTANCE: 1.8km (1.2miles) **ALLOW:** 1 hour

START

OBENCÍ DŮM
➕ G7 🚇 Náměstí Republiky

① From the Municipal House, go along Celetná, then turn right into the courtyard of No.17. This leads you into Štupartská, then into Malá Štupartská to the baroque façade of St. James's church.

② Go back a few steps, turning right under the archway into Týn Court. Leave by the far entrance and go along the side of the Týn church into Old Town Square.

③ Leaving the Town Hall on your right, continue into Malé náměstí (Little Square). Turn right, then left into Mariánské náměstí (Marian Square).

④ Go left out of the square along Husová, passing on the left the Clam-Gallas palace with its muscular atlantes.

END

NOVOTNÉHO LÁVKA
➕ E7 🚇 Staroměstská

⑧ Walk along the river toward Charles Bridge, turning left along the pier. End your walk at Smetana's statue.

⑦ Cross the square into the alley-way leading to Náprstkova; turn right. At the end of the street, go up the steps facing you on the landward side. Use the crossing to the left to cross the busy road to the riverside.

⑥ Continue in the same direction along Anenská, turning left into Anenské náměstí (Agnes Square). The square houses the Theatre at the Balustrade, where Václav Havel began his theatrical career.

⑤ Plunge through the crowds thronging the Royal Way and continue a short distance along Husová, turning right into narrow Řetězová.

WALK

Shopping

AGHARTA

Jazz, jazz and more jazz on sale at this popular nightspot.

🗓 F7 ✉ Železná 16
☎ 222 211 275
🕐 Evenings only 🚇 Můstek

ALMA ANTIQUE

Rambling, old-fashioned ground floor and basement establishment with every conceivable kind of antique object.

🗓 F7 ✉ Valentinská 7
☎ 222 325 865
🚇 Staroměstská

ANAGRAM

Fiction, philosophy, religion and history in English are the specialties of this bookshop located in the bustling Týn Courtyard.

🗓 G7 ✉ Týn 4 (between Týnská and Štupartská)
☎ 224 895 737 🚇 Náměstí Republiky

ANTIKVARIÁT KAREL KŘENEK

Antiquarian bookseller in the Obecní dům building but located around the back from the main entrance. You'll find an interesting selection of books, prints, old maps and lithographs.

🗓 G7 ✉ U Obecního domu 8 ☎ 222 314 734
🚇 Náměstí Republiky

ANTIKVARIÁT PAŘÍŽSKÁ

One of the few shops on this prestigious boulevard not to deal in designer labels and fashion, with walls papered with antique maps and prints.

🗓 F7 ✉ Pařížská 8 ☎ 222 321 442 🚇 Staroměstská

ART DECO

Lots of glass, ceramics, clothing, jewellery and more from the 1920s and '30s.

🗓 F7 ✉ Michalská 21
☎ 224 223 076 🚇 Národní třída

ARTĚL

High-end, functional reproduction glassware inspired by avant-garde Czech designs of the 1920s and '30s, as well as a unique selection of esoteric gift ideas. Owned and operated by an American expat with a fine eye for value and lovable kitsch.

🗓 G7 ✉ Celetná 29 (entrance on Rybná)
☎ 224 815 085 🚇 Náměstí Republiky

REPRODUCTIONS

Genuine art nouveau objects can be expensive, Cubist objects astronomically so. Superb, though far from cheap reproductions of the latter can be found in an appropriate setting on the ground floor of the Cubist Dům U Černé Matky Boží (Black Madonna House) at the eastern end of Celetná ✉ Ovocný trh 19.

BIG BEN BOOKSHOP

Guidebooks and Czech literature in translation are in good supply at this small, characterful shop.

🗓 G7 ✉ Malá Štupartská 5
☎ 224 826 565 🚇 Náměstí Republiky

BOHEME

Smart and simple women's fashion, with an emphasis on well-made, practical separates and accessories.

🗓 F6 ✉ Dušní 8 ☎ 224 813 840 🚇 Staroměstská

BOTANICUS

Organic products—soap, cosmetics, teas, herbs and spices—produced on a farm in Lysá nad Labem under the expert supervision of a British specialist.

🗓 F7 ✉ Týn 3 ☎ 234 767 446 🚇 Můstek

CELETNÁ CRYSTAL

Sells good-quality Bohemian glass.

🗓 G7 ✉ Celetná 15
☎ 222 324 022 🚇 Náměstí Republiky

COUNTRY LIFE

Healthy natural foods—elsewhere hard to find in this calorie-addicted city.

🗓 F7 ✉ Melantrichova 15
🚇 Můstek

CULINARIA

Well-stocked international delicatessen. A particular boon for those more enthusiastic about the culinary products of the Mediterranean lands than those of Central Europe.

🔲 F8 ✉ Skořepka 9
☎ 224 231 017 Ⓜ Národní třída/Můstek

DOROTHEUM

This branch of the long-established Vienna auction house has a fine range of antiques of all kinds. No bargains, but no ripoffs either.

🔲 G7 ✉ Ovocný trh 2
☎ 224 216 699 Ⓜ Můstek or Náměstí Republiky

GALERIE PEITHNER-LICHTENFELS

Modern Czech and Austrian art, including works from the period between the two world wars. The wide range of paintings, prints and sculptures makes a purchase possible for every pocket.

🔲 F7 ✉ Michalská 12
☎ 224 227 680 🚇 Můstek

GRANÁT

Bohemian garnets are world-famous; this factory shop has the most varied selection.

🔲 G6 ✉ Dlouhá 30
☎ 222 315 612 Ⓜ Náměstí Republiky

HAVELSKÝ TRH

Atmospheric market for fruits, vegetables and souvenirs. Prices are generally lower than in the shops.

🔲 F7 ✉ Staré Město
🕐 Daily Ⓜ Můstek

KOTVA

The Anchor was completed in 1975 to a Western-inspired 'brutalist' design and for a while was the city's foremost shopping site, although the range of goods would have been considered basic to Western consumers of the time.

🔲 G7 ✉ Náměstí Republiky 8 Ⓜ Náměstí Republiky

MANUFAKTURA

Natural goods and traditional handicrafts, including linens, blankets, hand-dyed fabrics, wooden toys and Christmas ornaments. Also a range of cosmetics and handmade soaps.

🔲 F7 ✉ Melantrichova 17
☎ 221 632 480 Ⓜ Můstek

MUSIC MISCELLANY

In addition to excellent CDs of music by the classical composers most closely associated with the city (Mozart, Dvořák, Smetana...), Prague shops stock highly individual pop music (Šum Svistu, or Laura and her Tigers, Psi vojáci...). Even more distinctive are the brass bands—the best you've ever heard—pumping out Czech (yes, Czech) old-time preferences such as 'Roll Out the Barrel' (Škoda lásky).

MODERNISTA

Fans of Cubist and early-Modern furniture design and decorative arts from the 1920s and '30s will want to pop in at the Celetná showroom. Most of the affordable pieces here are reproductions, but there are some lovingly restored originals here and there.

🔲 G7 ✉ Celetná 12
☎ 224 241 300 Ⓜ Náměstí Republiky

QUBUS

Quirky design and gift shop with bold designs of glassware and home furnishings. The place to come if you're looking for something truly unique.

🔲 G6 ✉ Rámová 3 ☎ 222 313 151 Ⓜ Staroměstská

TIMOURE ET GROUP

Chic and trendy women's fashion by two enterprising Czech graduates of the School of Applied Arts.

🔲 F/G6 ✉ V kolkovně 6
☎ 222 327 358
Ⓜ Staroměstská

VINO UNGELT

This well-stocked wine shop offers (for a fee) tastings from its huge range of Bohemian and Moravian vintages.

🔲 G7 ✉ Týn 7 ☎ 224 827 501 Ⓜ Náměstí Republiky

Entertainment and Nightlife

AGHARTA JAZZ CENTRUM

Cramped but enjoyable for local and international jazz, with cocktails and snacks. CD shop.
🞧 F7 ✉ Železná 16
☎ 222 211 275 🚇 Můstek

DIVADLO IMAGE (IMAGE THEATRE)

Visitor-oriented theatre with black light shows, featuring dance, mime and music.
🞧 F7 ✉ Pařížská 4 ☎ 222 314 448 🚇 Staroměstská

JAZZ CLUB U STARÉ PANÍ

Some of the best local musicians play in this central jazz club.
🞧 F7 ✉ Michalská 9
☎ 603 551 680 🚇 Můstek

KARLOVY LÁZNĚ

Self-proclaimed Central Europe's biggest club gets going around 11pm until dawn most nights.
🞧 E7/8 ✉ Smetanovo nábřeží 198 ☎ 222 220 502
🚇 Staroměstská

KLEMENTINUM

This vast complex (▷ 35) hosts chamber concerts in its Hall of Mirrors (Zrcadlová síň).
🞧 F7 ✉ Entrances at Karlova 1, Mariánské náměstí and Křižovnické náměstí
🚇 Staroměstská

NÁRODNÍ DIVADLO MARIONET (NATIONAL MARIONETTE THEATRE)

Adaptations of operas are among the attractions. There are matinees for youngsters.
🞧 F7 ✉ Žatecká 1 ☎ 224 819 322 🚇 Staroměstská

ROXY

Unusual underground establishment that has DJs and live acts of every conceivable stripe, including stars of world music.
🞧 G6 ✉ Dlouhá 33
☎ 224 826 296
🚇 Staroměstská

RUDOLFINUM

The Dvořák Hall of this splendid neo-Renaissance hall on the Vltava is the home of the Czech Philharmonic Orchestra. The Little (or Suk) Hall is used for chamber concerts.
🞧 F6 ✉ Náměstí Jana Palacha ☎ 227 059 227
🚇 Staroměstská

CINEMA

Czechs love the movies—both their own domestic productions as well as Hollywood blockbusters. Several of the old movie houses have survived. Look for the Lucerna cinema at the Lucerna shopping passage (▷ 58) and the Svûtozor cinema, which often plays Czech movies with English subtitles. The best multiplex is the Slovanský dům shopping mall (▷ 58). Check *The Prague Post* for full details.

SMETANOVA SÍŇ (SMETANA HALL)

www.fok.cz
Part of the sumptuously decorated Municipal House (▷ 30), and home of the first-class Prague Symphony Orchestra.
🞧 G7 ✉ Náměstí Republiky 5 ☎ 222 002 336
🚇 Náměstí Republiky

STAVOVSKÉ DIVADLO (ESTATES THEATRE)

The spectacular auditorium of this venue, with five tiers of box seats, is a wonderful setting for opera. Performances are at 7.30pm with matinees on weekends. Also ▷ 36.
🞧 G7 ✉ Ovocný trh 1
☎ 224 901 448 🚇 Můstek

TA FANTASTIKA

Another spectacle based on the black light fusion of dance, mime and music—a spin-off from the hugely successful Laterna Magika. The stage also hosts pop musicals starring local idols.
🞧 F7 ✉ Karlova 8
☎ 222 221 366
🚇 Staroměstská

UNGELT JAZZ 'N' BLUES CLUB

More pub than club, this newish place concentrates on local talent.
🞧 G7 ✉ Týn 2 (enter from Týnská ulička) ☎ 224 895 748 🚇 Staroměstská

Restaurants

PRICES

Prices are approximate, based on a 3-course meal for one person.

£££	over 800Kč
££	400Kč–800Kč
£	under 400Kč

ALLEGRO (£££)

The riverside restaurant of the Four Seasons Hotel has been voted the country's best for its high-quality Italian and traditional cooking. In 2008, Allegro snared the Czech Republic's first Michelin star.
🔢 F7 ✉ Veleslavínova 2a
☎ 221 427 000
Ⓜ Staroměstská

ANGEL (££–£££)

This beautifully turned out fusion restaurant skillfully links Asian ingredients and technique to local tastes.
🔢 G6 ✉ V Kolkovně 7
☎ 773 222 422
Ⓜ Staroměstská

BAKESHOP (£–££)

Possibly the best bakery and sandwich shop in Central Europe stocks a wide variety of freshly made soups and sandwiches, plus innovative salads. Good cakes, cookies and brownies.
🔢 G6 ✉ Kozí 1 ☎ 222 316 823 Ⓜ Staroměstská

BAROCK (££)

Trendy bar-restaurant well located on Prague's glitziest shopping street.
🔢 F6 ✉ Pařížská 24
☎ 222 329 221
Ⓜ Staroměstská

BELLEVUE (£££)

If dining with a view is what you're after, you can't do better than this. Ask for a window table looking out over the Vltava and Prague Castle in the distance. Great interior and high-quality international cuisine.
🔢 F6 ✉ Smetanovo nábřeží
☎ 222 221 443
Ⓜ Staroměstská 🚊 Tram 6, 9, 17, 18 to Národní divadlo

CHEZ MARCEL (£–££)

This comfy café/restaurant serves up typical French bistro fare. Popular among expats.
🔢 G6 ✉ Haštalská 12
☎ 222 315 676 🚊 Tram 5, 8, 14 to Dlouhá třída

TURKISH COFFEE

Espresso, cappuccino and most other coffees can now be found in Prague, but don't be surprised if you get served a traditional 'turecká káva'. This is Czech-style Turkish coffee—that is, hot water poured right over ground coffee. Invariably served in a piping-hot glass with no handle. Be sure to stop swallowing—that is before you disturb the deposit of coffee grounds at the bottom of the cup.

COUNTRY LIFE (£)

Healthy eating and food shopping in the heart of the Old Town. Closed Saturday.
🔢 F7 ✉ Melantrichova 15
☎ 224 213 366 Ⓜ Můstek

KING SOLOMON (£££)

Good kosher food and a lovely winter garden.
🔢 F7 ✉ Široka 8, Josefov
☎ 224 818 752
Ⓜ Staroměstská

KLUB ARCHITEKTŮ (£–££)

This romanesque cellar next to the Bethlehem chapel has vegetarian options, along with Czech staples served with a twist. English menus also available.
🔢 F8 ✉ Betlémské náměstí 5a ☎ 224 401 214
Ⓜ Národní třída

KOLKOVNA (£–££)

This updated take on the traditional pub, near Old Town Square, serves Czech staples along with pastas and salads. Great for groups, but be sure to reserve in advance.
🔢 F6 ✉ V Kolkovně 8
☎ 224 819 701
Ⓜ Staroměstská

PIZZA NUOVO (£–££)

If you're visiting with the kids, it's hard not to like an all-you-can-eat pizza and pasta menu, with an adjoining supervized play room for small children. The

pizzas are authentic—
from a Naples recipe.
The antipasto buffet is
very good value.
➕ G7 ✉ Revouncní 1
☎ 221 803 308 Ⓜ Náměstí
Republiky

PLZEŇSKÁ
RESTAURACE (££)

In the basement of
the Municipal House
(▷ 30–31) is this art nouveau designer's idea of
what a Bohemian beer
hall should look like. The
food is standard pub fare
such as goulash.
➕ G7 ✉ Náměstí
Republiky 5 ☎ 222 002 770
Ⓜ Náměstí Republiky

POTREFENÁ HUSA
(£)

This is one branch of
the 'Wounded Goose'—
bright, cheerful and very
contemporary bars with
satisfying Czech and
international food.
➕ F6 ✉ Bílkova 5 ☎ 222
326 626 Ⓜ Staroměstská

RYBÍ TRH (£££)

Sumptuous fish restau-
rant in the enchanting
Týn Court.
➕ G7 ✉ Týn 5 ☎ 224 895
447 Ⓜ Staroměstská,
Náměstí Republiky

SLAVIA (£)

This classic Central
European café, once the
haunt of dissident intel-
lectuals, has a superb
view over the Vltava.
➕ E8 ✉ Smetanovo
nábřeží 2 ☎ 224 218 493
Ⓜ Národní třída

U MEDVÍDKŮ (£)

Budvar, from the town
of České Budějovice in
southern Bohemia, is
probably the best-
known Bohemian beer
apart from Pilsener. Try
it on tap, in the garden,
in summer. New equip-
ment in 2008 makes for
even better beer on tap.
➕ F8 ✉ Na Perštýně 7
☎ 224 211 916 Ⓜ Národní
třída

VEGGIE REVOLUTION

Before 1989, vegetarians
venturing to Prague were
liable to be served endless
omelettes, perhaps with
extra dumplings. Czechs
still like their rich and
hearty meat-based dishes,
but the quality and range
of vegetarian offerings
continue to improve.

U MODRÉ
KACHNIČKY II (££)

The 'Blue Duckling II' is
an offshoot of the original
establishment in Malá
Strana (▷ 94). Both offer
a sophisticated take on
traditional Bohemian
cuisine, featuring succu-
lent game.
➕ F7 ✉ Michalská 16
☎ 224 213 418 Ⓜ Můstek

U VEJVODŮ (£)

This old pub has been
renovated, enlarged
and cleaned up, and
now the Pilsner palace
appeals to visitors and
locals alike.
➕ F7 ✉ Jilská 4 ☎ 224
219 999 Ⓜ Národní třída

Prague's commercial heart beats strongly in the New Town. The district is focused on a series of squares; foremost is Václavské náměstí, with Národní muzeum and the statue of Good King Wenceslas.

Map Labels

Vltava

- Karlovy lázně
- Náprstkova
- Náprstkovo muzeum
- Betlémská
- Konviktská
- Bartolomějská
- Pštrossova
- Národní třída
- krocinova
- sv Vorši
- Viola div
- Národní
- Ostrovní
- div Reduta
- Národní divadlo
- Laterna magika
- Masarykovo nábřeží
- most Legii
- V jirchářích
- Ostrovní
- Střelecký ostrov
- Žofín
- Na Struze
- Pštrossova
- Opatovická
- Černá
- Lazarská
- Slovanský ostrov
- Muzeum Piva
- sv Vojtěch
- Myslíkova
- Myslíkova
- Odbory
- Karlovo náměstí
- Mánes
- Jiráskovo nám.
- Svatého Cyril a Metoděj
- Dittrichova
- RESSLOVA
- Karlovo náměstí
- JIRÁSKŮV MOST
- Tančící dům
- ČVUT
- Gorazdova
- Trojanova
- Na Moráni
- Moráň
- Palackého náměstí
- Palackého most
- Palackého nám.
- sv Jan na skalce
- Na Moráni
- RAŠÍNOVO
- Dřevná
- Podskalská
- Trojická
- Vyšehradská
- klášter Na Slovanech (Emauzy)
- Botanická zahrada
- Nejsv Trojice
- Ladova
- Plavecká
- NÁBŘEŽÍ
- Horská
- Na Hrobci
- Na Hrobci
- Botičská
- Na Slupi
- Svobodova
- Výtoň
- Výtoň
- SVOBODOVA
- VNISLAVOVA
- Neklanova
- Libušina
- Vratislavova
- VYŠEHRAD
- sv Petra Pavel
- Vyšehrad
- rotunda
- Vyšehradské sady
- galerie
- Soběslavova
- Ústav pro péči o matku a dítě

Scale: 0 — 250 m / 0 — 250 yds

Muchovo muzeum

Advertising poster (left); detail of a window sculpture (below)

THE BASICS

www.mucha.cz
G7
Kaunický palác, Panská 7
224 216 415
Daily 10–6
Moderate
Můstek or Náměstí Republiky
Tram 3, 9, 14, 24 to Jindřišská

HIGHLIGHTS

● Sarah Bernhardt Gismonda poster
● Moravian Teachers' Choir poster
● Re-created Paris studio
● Biographical film

Best known for his posters of languorous Parisian lovelies advertising everything from champagne to cigarettes, art nouveau artist Alfons Mucha was a proud Czech patriot whose later work celebrated his country's independence.

From Alphonse to Alfons Alfons Mucha (1860–1939) was an émigré Czech who first found fame in Paris when he created a sensation with a stunning poster of the actress Sarah Bernhardt. Mucha was an idealist who hoped that art nouveau would break down the barriers between high art and everyday design. After his return to Prague, he worked on a variety of projects, from decorating the interiors of the Obecní dům (▷ 30) to designing stamps and banknotes for the new Czechoslovak Republic and stained glass for St. Vitus's Cathedral.

Museum exhibits Housed in the 18th-century Kaunic Palace, this museum shows off Mucha memorabilia, as well as drawings, paintings and sculpture, and an atmospheric re-creation of the Paris studio he shared with Rodin and Gauguin. In his later years, Mucha devoted himself to a sequence of 20 immense canvases depicting high points in the history of the Czechs and other Slav peoples. The paintings were intended to be put on permanent display in the capital, and although a Prague home is planned, they continue to languish in a provincial castle. The museum here shows an excellent English-language film about them.

Exterior views of the theatre, one reflected in a modern building (below)

Národní divadlo

Even if the thought of a classical play performed in Czech doesn't enthrall you, don't miss the National Theatre. It is, perhaps, the greatest of Prague's collective works of art, decorated by the finest artists of the age.

National drama Theatre in Prague still spoke with a German voice in the mid-19th century. Money to build a specifically Czech theatre was collected from 1849 onward, without support from Habsburg-dominated officialdom. The foundation stone was laid in 1868 with much festivity, then in 1881, shortly after the gala opening, the building burned down. Undiscouraged, the populace rallied, and by 1883 it had been completely rebuilt. The opening was celebrated with a grand gala performance of the opera *Libuše* by Smetana, a passionate supporter of the building's project.

Expanded ambition The National Theatre stands at the New Town end of Most Legií (Legions Bridge), its bulk carefully angled to fit into the streetscape and not diminish the view to Petřín Hill on the far bank. It was given a long-deserved restoration in time for its centenary, and when it reopened in 1983 it had gained a piazza and three annexes, whose architecture has been much maligned, the least unkind comment being that the buildings seem to be clad in bubble-wrap. Prague's popular multimedia show Laterna Magika (▷ 59) performs in one of the buildings, the Nová scéna.

THE BASICS

www.narodni-divadlo.cz
🔢 E8
✉ Národní 2
☎ 224 901 448
🍴 Bar
🚋 Tram 6, 9, 17, 18, 21, 22, 23 to Národní divadlo
♿ Few
🎟 Opera tickets: moderate–expensive

HIGHLIGHTS

● Bronze troikas above the entrance loggia
● Star-patterned roof of the dome
● Frescoes in the foyer by Mikoláš Aleš
● Painted ceiling of the auditorium, by František Ženíšek
● Painted stage curtain by Vojtěch Hynais
● View of the buiding from Střelecký Island
● Any performance of an opera from the Czech repertoire

NOVÉ MĚSTO

★ TOP 25

47

Národní muzeum

The spacious three-floor staircase; sculpture outside the museum

THE BASICS

www.nm.cz

➕ H9

✉ Václavské náměstí 68

☎ 224 497 111

🕐 May–end Sep daily 10–6; Oct–end Apr daily 9–5. Closed first Tue of month

🍴 Café

🚇 Muzeum

♿ Few

💰 Moderate; free first Mon of month

HIGHLIGHTS

● Allegorical sculptures on the terrace
● The Pantheon and dome
● Coin collection
● Collection of precious stones
● Skeleton of a whale

Some people find Prague's National Museum disappointing. However, try to enjoy it as a period piece in its own right, for its dusty showcases are as venerable as the building itself.

Top building With its gilded dome crowning the rise at the top of Václavské náměstí (Wenceslas Square, ▷ 50), Prague's National Museum provides a grand finale to the capital's most important street. The neo-Renaissance building was completed in 1891, and at the time was as much an object of pride to the Czech populace as the Národní divadlo (National Theatre, ▷ 47). Such is its presence that some visitors have mistaken it for the parliament building, as did the Soviet gunner who raked its façade with machine-gun fire in August 1968.

An array of -ologies Even if you are not a keen entomologist, paleontologist, zoologist, mineralogist or numismatist, you won't fail to be impressed by the evidence here of the 19th century's great passion for collecting and classifying. Efforts are under way to make the treasures here more accessible and entertaining; there are interactive displays, a schedule of often fascinating temporary exhibits, and a dinosaur display to engage the young. But above all, the building itself is impressive, with its grand stairways, statuary, mosaics and patterned floors. Unlike most attractions in Prague, it's open on Monday.

St. Martin's Rotunda
(below); the river and
Vyšehrad (right)

Vyšehrad

THE BASICS

www.praha-vysehrad.cz

🔒 F12

✉ Information area: V
Pevnosti, Vyšehrad. Brick
Gate: Vratislavova,
Vyšehrad

☎ 241 410 348

🕐 Prague Fortifications
Museum: Apr–end Oct
daily 9.30–6; Nov–end
Mar daily 9.30–5.
Cemetery: Apr–end Oct
daily 8–7; Nov–end Mar
daily 8–5

🍴 Restaurant

🚇 Vyšehrad

🚊 Trams 3, 7, 16, 17 to
Výtoň then steep uphill
walk

♿ Fair

💰 Park and cemetery: free
Museum: inexpensive

**Rising high above the River Vltava is
Vyšehrad (High Castle), where the
soothsaying Princess Libuše foresaw
the founding of Prague, and where she
married her ploughman swain, Přemysl.**

Romantic rock Beneath Vyšehrad's 19th-
century neo-Gothic Church of St. Peter and
St. Paul are the remains of a far earlier,
Romanesque church that once served the royal
court. But it was in the 19th century, with the
rise of Romantic ideas about history and nation-
hood, that poets, playwrights and painters
celebrated the great fortress-rock, elaborating
the story of Libuše. Most of their efforts have
been forgotten, though Smetana's 'Vyšehrad',
part of his glorious tone-poem *Má Vlast*, remains
popular. The nation's great and good have been
buried in the National Cemetery (or Pantheon) at
Vyšehrad since the late 19th century. Smetana
himself is here, and fellow composer Dvořák.
On the lawns nearby are freestanding sculptures
of Libuše and other legendary figures by Josef
Václav Myslbek, the creator of the St.
Wenceslas statue in Wenceslas Square.

Vltava views Everyone driving along the
main riverside highway has to pay homage to
Vyšehrad, as the road and tram tracks twist
and turn and then tunnel through the high rock
protruding into the Vltava. In the 1920s the
whole hilltop was turned into a public park,
with wonderful views up and down the river
(▷ 52).

HIGHLIGHTS

● National Cemetery
graves and memorials and
the Slavín mausoleum
● St. Martin's Rotunda
(Romanesque church)
● Cihelná brána (Brick
Gate), with Prague
Fortifications Museum
● Ramparts walk
● Neo-Gothic Kostel sv
Petra a Pavla (Church of
St. Peter and St. Paul)

Václavské náměstí

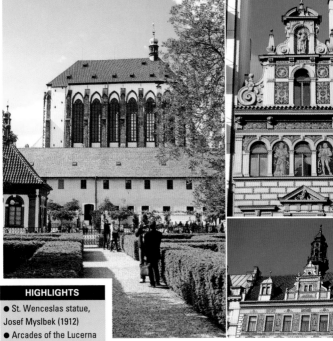

Despite its sometimes rather seedy air, Wenceslas Square is still the place where the city's heart beats most strongly, and to meet someone 'beneath the horse' (the Wenceslas statue) remains a thrill.

When is a square not a square? When it's a boulevard. 'Václavák', 700m (763 yards) long, slopes gently up to the imposing façade of the National Museum (▷ 48). Just down the slope stands the statue of 'Good King' Wenceslas on his sprightly steed, a good place for a rendezvous at any time of day and night.

History in the making Many dramas of modern times have been played out in Wenceslas Square. The new state of Czechoslovakia was proclaimed here in 1918, and in 1939 German

Clockwise from left: Františkánská zahrada or Franciscan Garden, reached via the arcades of the Palac Alfa; sgraffito façade on a building; advertisement on top of building on the corner of Vodičkova and Václavské náměstí; classical statues support a bay window on No. 8 Václavské náměstí; Wiehluv dům (exterior views)

tanks underlined the republic's demise. In 1968, more tanks arrived—this time to crush the Prague Spring of Alexander Dubček. To protest at the Soviet occupation, Jan Palach burned himself to death here in 1969, and in 1989 Dubček and Václav Havel waved from the balcony of No. 36 as Czechs crowded here to celebrate the collapse of Communism.

Museum of modern architecture The procession of buildings lining both sides of the square, from the resplendent art nouveau Hotel Evropa to the elegant Functionalist Bat'a Store, tells the story of the Czech contribution to 20th-century architecture and design. More intriguing are the arcades that burrow deep into the buildings, creating a labyrinth of boutiques, entertainment venues, cafés and cinemas.

THE BASICS

✚ G–H8
✉ Václavské náměstí
🍽 Many restaurants and cafés
🚇 Můstek or Muzeum
♿ Fair

TIP

● People-watching on the square can be accomplished from the terrace cafés on the east side, which catch the midday and afternoon sun.

Vltava Boat Trip

TOP 25

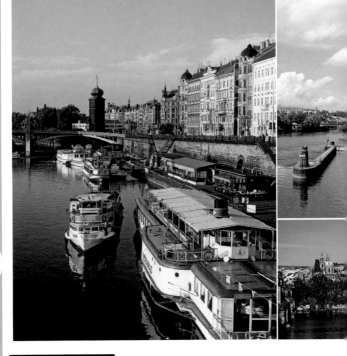

A cruise is a wonderful way to see Prague from a different angle. Some of the bridges are works of art, and there are many other fascinating river sights immortalized by Bedřich Smetana.

National river The Vltava (sometimes known by its German name of Moldau) rises high in the hills along the Austrian border. Flowing north into the Elbe (Labe in Czech) some 40km (25 miles) downstream from Prague, its waters eventually discharge into the North Sea. Mostly tranquil, the river's mood can change suddenly; its banks have often burst, and in 1890 it swept away several of the arches of Charles Bridge. Dams upstream were supposed to have tamed it, but failed to prevent the disastrous flood of August 2002, when much of

Clockwise from the left: large river boats cruise the Vltava, overlooked by the row of buildings, which line Masaryk Embankment; the Vltava; a couple in a small row boat passing a swan; mature trees obscure some of the colour-washed façades of the buildings on the riverbank, with the towers of St. Vitus's Cathedral behind

Malá Strana, Smíchov, Karlín and the cellars of Staré Město were inundated. Despite such incidents, it's the most loved of Czech rivers.

Riverside delights Several operators run boat trips down the Vltava that are an especially fun way to spend an afternoon or evening. Most of the boats leave from the embankment just below Čechův most (the Čechův bridge, near the Hotel Intercontinental) and cruise upstream to beyond Charles Bridge and on to near Vyšehrad before turning back. Cruises run year-around, though summer is obviously a better bet for suitable weather and offers more of a choice among different cruises. The main operator is Evropská vodní doprava (EVD) (▷ panel), but tours can be booked through many different travel agencies.

THE BASICS

Evropská vodní doprava
www.evd.cz
✉ Quay at Cechuv
☎ 224 810 030
⊙ Year-round, though more frequent departures in summer
▨ Moderate–expensive
❓ Useful websites for cruises:
www.pragueexperience.com
www.cruise-prague.cz
www.myczechrepublic.com

More to See

KARLOVO NÁMĚSTÍ

Karlovo náměstí (Charles Square) is more of a park than a square, and is a useful resting place when pounding the pavements becomes too tiring in this spread-out part of town.
➕ F9

MUZEUM HLAVNÍHO MĚSTA PRAHY (CITY MUSEUM)

www.muzeumprahy.cz

This late 19th-century building contains exhibits telling the story of Prague's evolution from the earliest times. The star is a scale model of the city as it was in the 1820s and 1830s. Most of the extensive collections are in storage, but selections are shown in rotation.
➕ J6 ✉ Na Poříčí 52, north Nové Město ☎ 224 816 773 🕐 Tue–Sun 9–6 🚇 Florenc 💰 Inexpensive

MUZEUM KOMUNISMU

www.museumofcommunism.com

The Museum of Communism is a private venture, which has attracted much controversy. The museum contrasts Communism's Utopian dreams with the grim reality of empty shops, meaningless slogans and pervasive policing. An upbeat note is struck at the end, however, with a short film about the Velvet Revolution, which brought an end to the oppressive regime.
➕ G7 ✉ Na Příkopě 10 ☎ 224 212 966 🕐 Daily 9–9 💰 Adult moderate, child free 🚇 Můstek

MUZEUM POLICIE ČR (POLICE MUSEUM)

www.mvcr.cz

This museum recovered quickly from the collapse of the old order in 1989 and gives an upbeat account of Czech policing, with lots of gore and weaponry on show in what was once a monastery.
➕ G11 ✉ Ke Karlovu 1 ☎ 224 922 183 🕐 Tue–Sun 10–5 🚇 I P Pavlova or Vyšehrad 💰 Inexpensive

PANNY MARIE SNĚŽÉ

The great Gothic Church of Our Lady of the Snows was intended by

Novoměstská radnice (Town Hall) on Karlovo náměstí

Carved figures inside the Church of Our Lady of the Snows

Emperor Charles IV to rival St. Vitus's Cathedral and to dominate the skyline of the New Town. But the Hussite Troubles ended building work, and only the chancel was completed. The best view of the exterior is from the Franciscans' Garden. The interior demonstrates both Gothic mastery of space and baroque determination not to be outdone.

🔲 G8 ✉ Jungmannovo náměstí 18 ☎ 224 490 350 🕐 Mon–Sat 9–5.15, Sun 12.30–5.15 (no visiting during Mass) 🎫 Free 🚇 Můstek 🚋 Tram 6, 9, 18, 21, 22, 23 to Národní třída

POŠTOVNÍ MUZEUM

www.cpost.cz

The national collection of stamps and postal memorabilia is housed in a 16th-century building with original painted interiors. The emphasis is on stamps from Czechoslovakia and its successor republics, but there's much else besides.

🔲 G6 ✉ Nové mlýny 2 ☎ 222 312 006 🕐 Tue–Sun 9–12, 1–5 🎫 Inexpensive 🚋 Tram 5, 8, 14 to Dlouhá třída

SVATÉHO CYRIL A METODĚJ

On 18 June 1942, the Baroque Church of Saints Cyril and Methodius was where the Czechoslovak parachutists who had assassinated Reichsprotektor Reinhard Heydrich made their last stand. Their hiding place in the crypt betrayed by a former comrade, they valiantly held SS troops at bay with a hail of bullets for several hours. Finally, the fire brigade was ordered to flush them out by pumping in water. Rather than fall into the hands of a merciless enemy, the defenders used their last bullets on themselves. Their heroism, and that of the churchmen who hid them, is commemorated by a plaque outside the church and by displays in the crypt itself.

🔲 F9 ✉ Resslova 9 ☎ 224 920 686 🕐 May–end Sep Tue–Sun 10–5; Oct–end Apr Tue–Sun 10–4 🎫 Inexpensive 🚇 Karlovo náměstí 🚋 Tram 3, 4, 6, 7, 10, 14, 16, 17, 18, 21, 22, 23, 24 to Karlovo náměstí

A display in the museum housed in the Vila Amerika (▷ 60)

Exterior of the Statni Opera Praha (Opera House; ▷ 60)

The Old and New

This route takes you along the bustling boulevards laid out along the dividing line between the Old and New Towns.

DISTANCE: 1.75km (just over a mile) **ALLOW:** 45 minutes

START

OBECNÍ DŮM
➕ G7 🅜 Náměstí Republiky

1 Turn right and walk along Na Příkopě. Now one of Prague's main shopping streets, it divides—or links—the Old and New Towns.

2 Pause to look inside the ornate Živnostenská banka (Napřikopě 20), built in 1896. In contrast on the north side of the street is the sober Komerční banka of 1908.

3 The point where Na Příkopě joins Wenceslas Square is called Můstek, or 'Little Bridge'.

4 Walk up the right-hand side of Wenceslas Square, and turn right into the old Alfa passage (Václavské náměstí 28) leading into the land-scaped Franciscans' Garden.

END

NÁRODNI DIVADLO
➕ E8 🚊 Tram: 6, 9, 17, 18, 21, 22, 23

8 Národní třída ends at the Národní divadlo (National Theatre). Opposite the building is the famous Café Slavia.

7 Continue along the left-hand side of Národní třída. In the arcade of No.16 there's a reminder of the Velvet Revolution, a little memorial commemorating the victims of police brutality.

6 Go past the statue of Josef Jungmann into Národní třída (National Avenue), laid out like Na Příkopě along the line of the Old Town ramparts.

5 Leave the garden via the far corner into Jungmannovo náměstí.

Shopping

ACADEMIA
Good variety of photography books, travel guides, cookbooks and literature in English.
G8 ✉ Václavské náměstí 34 ☎ 224 223 511 🚇 Můstek

ANTIKVARIÁT GALERIE MŮSTEK
This old-established firm in the arcade of the Adria Palace is a typical example of the Prague *antikvariát* (antiquarian bookshop), with not just books but an intriguing selection of maps, prints and a range of ephemera.
G8 ✉ Národní třída 40 ☎ 224 949 587 🚇 Můstek/Národní třída

BONTONLAND
This is reputedly the biggest music shop in Central Europe. The pop and rock section is vast, classical hardly less so. And there are DVDs and games galore. It is in the labyrinthine basement of the Koruna Palace at the corner of Wenceslas Square and Na příkopě.
G6/7 ✉ Václavské náměstí 1 ☎ 224 473 080 🚇 Můstek

CELLARIUS
In the Lucerna arcade off Wenceslas Square, this well-stocked shop sells wines from around the world as well from the vineyards of Bohemia and Moravia.

G8 ✉ Štěpánská 61 ☎ 224 210 979 🚇 Můstek

CENTRUM FOTOŠKODA
This place is a paradise for camera buffs, stocking every possible kind of photographic equipment (new and secondhand) as well as books and magazines.
G8 ✉ Vodičkova 37 ☎ 222 929 038 🚇 Můstek

DŮM PORCELÁNU
Very good selection of Czech-made porcelain from outlets in Western Bohemia at prices that are aimed at the local market—not tourists.
H9 ✉ Jugoslávská 16 ☎ 221 505 320 🚇 I P Pavlova

MALL MAGIC
The arrival of Western-style malls has transformed the shopping scene in Prague. With their bright and shiny, if not innovative, architecture and interior design they are a world away from the sterile and lifeless state-run department stores under communism. As a visitor, you won't want to spend too much time at the malls, still they are useful for picking up items you might have left at home. The biggest—and glitziest—mall in Prague is Palladium at Náměstí Republiky 1 (▷ 58).

ELAZAR
The Prague outlet of this venerable maker of fine clothes and accessories in fur and leather is on the ground floor of the Černá Růže arcade.
G7 ✉ Na Příkopě12 ☎ 224 214 835 🚇 Můstek

GLOBE BOOKSTORE AND COFFEEHOUSE
A congenial home-away-from-home for Americans and anyone hungry for literature in English, as well as light meals.
F9 ✉ Pštrossova 6 ☎ 224 934 203 🚇 Národní třída or Karlovo náměstí

HATLE ANTIKVARIÁT
Tucked away in a side-street a short distance from Wenceslas Square, this is another fine if dusty example of the Prague *antikvariát*.
G8 ✉ Palackého 9 ☎ 224 947 727 🚇 Můstek/Národní třída

HODINÁŘSTVÍ MATOUŠ
Beautiful antique clocks and watches.
F8 ✉ Mikulandská 10 ☎ 224 930 172 🚇 Národní třída

KIWI
A travel agency, plus this establishment has a comprehensive range of maps and guides to the Czech Republic and beyond. Hanging on the walls in the basement is

a fascinating collection of excellent maps.
🔲 G8 ✉ Jungmannova 23 ☎ 224 948 455 🅰 Národní třída

KLIMENT

Czechs are known for their love of music, from classical to pop, and here is where they buy their instruments. One of the best selections in the city.
🔲 G8 ✉ Jungmannova 17 ☎ 224 213 966 🅰 Můstek

LUCERNA PASSAGE

How shopping centers used to look in the 1920s—fun, elegant and filled with character. There's not actually much to buy here aside from some small gift stores and camera shops, but that makes it all the better. There's a big period-piece cinema, two excellent cafés and one of the best-known music clubs in the city. Worth seeking out.
🔲 G7 ✉ Štěpánska 61 ☎ 224 224 537 🅰 Můstek/ Muzeum

MOSER

A palatial first-floor outlet for the fine crystal and porcelain made in Carlsbad (Karlový Vary), along with porcelain from Meissen and Herend. No bargains, but objects of the highest quality are beautifully displayed here.
🔲 G7 ✉ Na Příkopě 12

☎ 224 211 293 🅰 Můstek or Náměstí Republiky

MYSLIVOST

This shop caters to that army of Czechs who love the outdoor life. Unusual weatherproof wear and much else.
🔲 G8 ✉ Jungmannova 25 ☎ 224 949 014 🅰 Národní třída

ORIGINAL SOUVENIR

Small but good-value souvenir shop near the bottom of Wenceslas Square featuring authentic Czech-made handicrafts.
🔲 G8 ✉ Václavské náměstí 12 ☎ No phone 🅰 Můstek

PALÁC KNIH LUXOR

There's no reason to dispute the claim of the 'Palace of Books' to be the biggest in the country. Descend to the basement for books in English and other foreign languages. The firm has another size-

able store in the Nový Smíchov mall.
🔲 G8 ✉ Václavské náměstí 41 ☎ 221 111 370 🅰 Můstek/Muzeum

PALLADIUM

The most recent super-sized mall to open, in late 2007, is the biggest and glitziest thing the Czech Republic has ever seen. Floor after floor of every kind of shop imaginable and a food court that seems to stretch on and on. Don't come looking for bargains though, the prices are sky high.
🔲 G/H7 ✉ Náměstí Republiky 1 ☎ 225 770 250 🅰 Náměstí Republiky

SLOVANSKÝ DŮM

Another shopping mall —just down the street from Palladium—but much more relaxed and manageable. Check out the restaurant Kogo and the multiplex cinema.
🔲 G7 ✉ Na Příkopě 22 ☎ 221 451 400 🅰 Můstek

TESCO

Rival to Kotva (▷ 39) and once bearing the impeccably proletarian name of 'Máj' (May), this department store is now in British hands. A ride up the escalator gives an excellent view of downtown. The basement supermarket is one of the best in town.
🔲 F8 ✉ Národní 26 ☎ 222 003 111 🅰 Národní třída

Entertainment and Nightlife

ČERNÉ DIVADLO JIŘÍHO SRNCE (JIŘÍ SRNEC BLACK THEATRE)

Legends of magic Prague presented in multimedia format. Jiří Srnec was the originator of black light cinema some 40 years ago.
✚ F8 ✉ Divadlo Reduta, Národní třída 20 ☎ 257 921 835 Ⓜ Národní třída

DIVADLO ARCHA (ARCHA THEATRE)

The Archa Theatre reaches out to non-Czech speakers with a fascinating avant-garde agenda of drama, dance, music and multi-media productions. Tickets for most shows are inexpensive and highly sought after—so book ahead.
✚ H6 ✉ Na Poříčí 26 ☎ 221 716 333 Ⓜ Náměstí Republiky

DIVADLO MINOR (MINOR THEATRE)

This well-known puppetry and drama ensemble puts on a varied schedule designed to appeal to children.
✚ G9 ✉ Vodičkova 6 ☎ 222 231 351 Ⓜ Můstek

DIVADLO PONEC

Contemporary dance theatre with an innovative schedule, based in a building in the district of Žižkov, just outside the New Town.
✚ J7 ✉ Husitská 24A ☎ 222 721 531 Ⓜ Florenc

HUDEBNÍ DIVADLO KARLÍN

Operettas and musicals are the undemanding fare in this suburban theatre just beyond the inner city. Although badly damaged by the 2002 flood, the Karlín Music Theatre is fully operational again, offering such spectacles as a complete Czech version of Mel Brooks's *The Producers*.
✚ J6 ✉ Křižíkova 10, Karlín ☎ 221 868 666 Ⓜ Florenc

HYBERNIA

A theatre in a former monastery aimed squarely at the tourist market with multilingual musicals like a recent performance of the Golem. The quality of the performances is high and a fun evening is virtually guaranteed.
✚ G7 ✉ Náměstí Republiky 4 ☎ 221 419 419 Ⓜ Náměstí Republiky

ROCK CZECH-STYLE

Before 1989, groups like the Plastic People of the Universe were seen as genuinely subversive of the existing order and were relentlessly hounded by State Security. Nowadays, the rock scene is a confused one, with a lot of fairly mindless imitation of Western trends but plenty of innovation, too.

LATERNA MAGIKA

The Magic Lantern's synthesis of film, music, theatre and mime was developed in the 1950s by Alfréd Radok, and continues to intrigue and delight audiences. Some of the most successful shows are reworkings of ancient myths.
✚ F8 ✉ Nová scéna of the National Theatre, Národní 4 ☎ 224 931 482 Ⓜ Národní třída

LUCERNA MUSIC BAR

This is part of the vast complex of the Lucerna Palace, a labyrinth of arcades and passageways that were the work of President Havel's builder-grandfather. Its good-sized ballroom can accommodate visiting groups as well as locals, and although some expats look down on it, it's the place to go for Czech retro.
✚ G8 ✉ Vodičkova 36 ☎ 224 217 108

METROPOLITAN JAZZ CLUB

Swing, ragtime and blues at this well-established and popular jazz club.
✚ G8 ✉ Jungmannova 14 ☎ 224 947 777 Ⓜ Národní třída or Můstek

NÁRODNÍ DIVADLO

The magnificent auditorium of the National

Theatre is *the* place in which to soak up well-staged performances of such classics from the Czech operatic repertoire as *The Bartered Bride* or *The Cunning Little Vixen*. The schedule also features foreign operas, ballet and drama.
✚ E8 ✉ Národní 2 ☎ 224 901 448 🚇 Národní třída

PALÁC AKROPOLIS
The best club in Prague for live rock, house and world music is not in Nové Město but farther afield in the up-and-coming but still-rough-in-spots district of Žižkov.
✚ Off map ✉ Kubelíková 27 ☎ 296 330 911 🚇 Jiřího z Poděbrad

RADOST FX
One of the most popular spots in town, this club in a street behind the National Museum has been packing them in ever since it was established in the early 1990s.
✚ H9 ✉ Bělehradská 120 ☎ 224 254 776 🚇 I P Pavlova

REDUTA
Bill Clinton blew his sax at this best-known of Prague jazz locales during his presidential visit to Prague in 1994. Hear dixieland, swing and modern jazz.
✚ F8 ✉ Národní 20 ☎ 224 933 487 🚇 Národní třída

ROCK CAFÉ
This downtown café

and concert spot is the place to go if you like your rock music hard and very loud.
✚ F8 ✉ Národní 20 ☎ 224 933 947 🚇 Národní třída

STÁTNÍ OPERA PRAHA (PRAGUE STATE OPERA)
Originally built in 1888 by Prague's German community as a rival to the exclusively Czech National Theatre, the State Opera has a reputation for more innovative productions of opera, ballet and drama.
✚ H8 ✉ Wilsonova 4 ☎ 224 227 266 🚇 Muzeum

VAGON
Popular rock venue that's heavy on heavy metal and revival acts, like the local talent Red Hot Chili Peppers Revival band.
✚ F8 ✉ Národní 25 ☎ 221 085 599 🚇 Národní třída

VILA AMERIKA
This miniature baroque palace now houses a museum devoted to the

talented composer Antonín Dvořák. There are chamber concerts in its elegant salon, and during the season it makes a lovely setting for an evening show featuring Dvořák's music.
✚ G10 ✉ Ke Karlovu 20 ☎ 224 918 013 🚇 I P Pavlova

KEEPING YOU POSTED
Since 1989 there has been a boom in performances of all kinds intended to appeal to foreign visitors. Posters and leaflets will keep you up to date about what's on, as will the English-language Prague Post weekly newspaper.

Restaurants

PRICES

Prices are approximate, based on a 3-course meal for one person.

fff   over 800Kč
ff   400Kč–800Kč
f   under 400Kč

ALCRON (fff)

Hands down, Prague's premier location for seafood. Elegant setting and intimate atmosphere in one of the eating places in the lavishly refurbished hotel of the same name.
🔹 G8 ✉ Štepánská 40 (in the Radisson SAS Alcron) ☎ 222 820 000 🕐 Dinner only, closed Sun 🚇 Muzeum

BRASSERIE M (ff)

Upscale, mostly smoke-free French brasserie, focusing on simple, classic dishes done well. One of a handful of Prague restaurants to win a 'bib gourmand' mention in the 2008 Michelin guide, meaning decent food for the money.
🔹 F8 ✉ Vladíslavová 17 ☎ 224 054 070 🚇 Národní třída

CAFÉ LOUVRE (f)

A famous establishment now under its original name, the Louvre is decorated in rococo style and offers everything from breakfast to billiards. Also a non-smoking room.

Voted café of the year in the columns of the *Prague Post*.
🔹 F8 ✉ Národní 22 ☎ 224 930 949 🚇 Národní třída

ČERNÝ KOHOUT (ff–fff)

High-standard traditional Czech cooking at prices to match. Good choice for a splurge. The *suma-va* lamb chops roasted in thyme come highly recommended. A three-course business luncheon menu offers many of the same great dishes at a third of the price.
🔹 F9 ✉ Vojtěšská 9 ☎ 251 681 191 🚇 Karlovo náměstí

DON PEDRO'S (f–ff)

Something a little different for Prague: a Colombian restaurant, serving a range of Latin American and Mexican

CZECH WINES AND SPIRITS

Although little known abroad, Czech wines are improving, especially both reds and whites from Moravia, and make an interesting souvenir. Spirits are cheap and often excellent. Slivovice (plum brandy) is well known, a supposed cure for all ills, while Becherovka, prepared in Carlsbad to a secret recipe, combines bitter and sweet tastes.

dishes in a fun, informal atmosphere. Burritos, *empanadas*, rice and beans, they're all here.
🔹 F9 ✉ Masarykovo nábřeží 2 ☎ 224 923 505 🚇 Národní třída

GOVINDA VEGETARIAN CLUB (f)

Plenty of whole food at this Hare Krishna restaurant/bakery/tea room, in a convenient location not far from the art nouveau Obecní dům (Municipal House, ▷ 30–31).
🔹 H6 ✉ Soukenicka 27 ☎ 603 205 991 🕐 Mon–Fri 11–5 🚇 Náměstí Republiky

KAVÁRNA EVROPA (f)

The art nouveau interior of the café attached to the famous Evropa Hotel is one of the sights of Prague, though service has not always matched the surroundings and at times an entrance fee has been charged.
🔹 G8 ✉ Václavské náměstí 25 ☎ 224 215 387

NOVOMĚSTSKÝ PIVOVAR (f–ff)

This brewery serves up its own light and dark lagers along with traditional Czech fare.
🔹 G8/9 ✉ Vodičkova 20 ☎ 222 231 662 🕐 Also open for breakfast Mon–Fri 🚋 Tram 3, 9, 14, 24 to Vodičkova

61

LA PERLE DE PRAGUE (£££)

Atop the controversial 'Fred and Ginger' building, sophisticated, mostly French food, with city and river views.

F9 ⊠ Rašínovo nábřeží 80 ☎ 221 984 160 🇶 Karlovo náměstí

PIVOVARSKÝ DŮM (£–££)

Get's very packed but this microbrewery is worth trying for its creative spin on the national beverage, beer—try coffee flavoured or sour cherry. Good food like roast pork and goulash. Book ahead.

G9 ⊠ Lípová 15 ☎ 296 216 666 🇶 I P Pavlova

POD KŘÍDLEM (££)

Stylish surroundings and impeccable Continental cuisine, with duck, pork and veal dishes. Also close to the National Theatre.

F8 ⊠ Národní 10 (entrance on Voršilská) ☎ 224 951 741 🇶 Národní třída

U FLEKŮ (££)

Highly popular with tour buses, but shouldn't dissaude you from trying the dark and tasty beer that has been brewed and served on these premises for 500 years. There's also a big beer garden.

F9 ⊠ Křemencova 11 ☎ 224 934 019 🇶 Národní třída

U KALICHA (££)

Thanks to the Good Soldier Švejk's patronage in Austro-Hungarian days, this place is popular with visitors from abroad familiar with the famous Czech antihero. Solid food and accordion music among much Švejkian memorabilia.

G10 ⊠ Na Bojišti 12–14 ☎ 224 912 557 🇶 I P Pavlova

UNIVERSAL (£)

A cross between a French bistro and a traditional Czech *hospoda* (pub), with salads and pasta dishes, as well as traditional and international main courses.

F9 ⊠ V jirchářích 6 ☎ 224 918 182 🇶 Národní třída

U PAŘAŠUTISTŮ (£–££)

World War II buffs will love this pub, a shrine to the Czechoslovak parachutists who assassinated Reichsprotektor Heydrich. Across the street is the museum devoted to them, located in the Sts. Cyril and Methodius Orthodox church.

EXOTIC TASTES

The Lemon Leaf (£–££) is a good choice for Thai and international cuisine. It is a short walk from Karlovo náměstí. ⊠ Na Zderaze 14 ☎ 224 919 056 🇶 Karlovo náměstí

F9 ⊠ Resslova 7 ☎ 737 670 278 🇶 Karlovo náměstí

U PINKASŮ (£–££)

This authentically restored pub was the first place in Prague to serve real Pilsner (in 1843). Refined dining is upstairs, in what is one of the very best places to enjoy sustaining Bohemian specialties such as tasty roast duck.

G8 ⊠ Jungmannovo náměstí 16 ☎ 221 111 150 🇶 Můstek

U ŠUTERŮ (££)

A cozy place specializing in Czech treats like roast duck, roast pork and fruit dumplings.

G8 ⊠ Palackého 4, Nové Město ☎ 224 948 235 🇶 Můstek

VELRYBA (£)

Popular student café with a relaxed intellectual vibe, good coffee and light meals.

F9 ⊠ Opatovická 24 ☎ 224 931 444 🇶 Národní třída

ZAHRADA V OPEŘE (££)

The place to dine after attending the Státní opera. Bright ambience, and delicious dishes from around the world.

H8 ⊠ Legerova 75 (across highway between Národní Muzeum and Státní Opera) ☎ 224 239 685 🇶 Muzeum

Hradčany takes its name from Prague Castle (Pražský hrad), the crag-topping citadel commanding the bridges of the River Vltava. The district extends along the hilltop to Strahovský klášter.

4

5

Na valech

U Prašného
mostu

Mariánské hradby

Minist
Obrany

Jeleni

Pražský
hrad

Královská
zahrada

Oranžerie

Brusnice

HRADČANY

Jízdárna
Praž hradu

U Brusnice

Jelení

Jiřský
klášter

Nový Svět

Brusnice

Bazilika a
klášter sv Jiří

6

Nový Svět

Šternberský
palác

Kanovnická

Katedrála
sv Víta

Černínská

sv Jan
Nepomucký

Martinický
palác

Pražský
hrad

Všech
svatých

Kapucínská

U Kasáren

Loreta

Hradčanské
náměstí

Arcibiskupský
palác

Starý
králový
palác

Keplerova

Černínský
palác

Loretánské
náměstí

Schwarzenberský
palác

Ke Hradu

Zám schody

Hládkov

Loretánská

Nerudova

Keplerova

Parléřova

Pohořelec

Úvoz

Lobkovická
zahrada

Pohořelec

7

Dlabačov

Strahovská

Strahovský
klášter

Strahovská
zahrada

8

0   250 m

0   250 yds

B

C

Interior and exterior views of the Basilica of St. George

Bazilika a klášter sv Jiří

A blood-red baroque façade conceals a severe ancient interior, the Romanesque Basilica of St. George. The nuns have long since left their convent to the north, now a setting for the National Gallery's collecton of Czech art of the 19th century.

Bare basilica The basilica is the biggest church of its date in the Czech provinces and its twin towers and pale, sober stonework are a reminder of the great antiquity of the Prague Castle complex. Very well preserved, it is now a concert venue. The austere interior, a great hall with wooden ceiling, houses a small but impressive collection of artworks.

Paintings and princesses Founded in 973, St. George's Convent was where princesses and other noble young ladies were sent for the best possible education. Shut down like many religious houses in 1782 by Emperor Joseph (who turned it into a barracks), it had to await the coming of the Communists for its rehabilitation; they planned to turn it into a museum of the Czechoslovak people. It now houses the new National Gallery collection of Czech art of the 19th century. The holdings focus on paintings and sculpture of the early 19th century and their links with the 18th century. Eventually the plan is for the collection to move and for the convent to hold a permanent collection of Gothic art.

HIGHLIGHTS

Basilica

● Gothic tomb of Prince Vratislav I

● St. Ludmila's chapel with frescoes

● Renaissance south portal

Katedrála sv Víta

HIGHLIGHTS

- South Portal, with 14th-century mosaic
- St. Wenceslas's Chapel
- Crypt, with royal tombs
- Silver tomb of St. John Nepomuk
- West front sculptures

TIP

- You can get some idea of the glories of the cathedral by walking along the nave, which is free. To see its greatest treasures, like St. Wenceslas's Chapel, you will need to buy a general castle admission ticket.

To emerge into Prague Castle's Third Courtyard and see the twin towers of St. Vitus's Cathedral lancing skyward is truly breathtaking. The sight is all the more compelling when you realize that this Gothic edifice was completed within living memory.

Spanning the centuries The cathedral was begun by Emperor Charles IV in the mid-14th century. It is built over the foundations of much earlier predecessors: a round church erected by 'Good King' (actually Prince) Wenceslas in the early 10th century and a big Romanesque building resembling the present-day Bazilika sv Jiří (▷ 67). The glory of the architecture is largely due to the Swabian builder Petr Parléř and his sons, who worked on the building for 60 years.

Clockwise from the left: detail of the Alfons Mucha art nouveau stained-glass window; the silver tomb of St. John Nepomuk; the spires of the cathedral dominate the rooftops of the Hradčany; the arched ceiling of the Chapel of the Holy Cross; exterior; bronze chandelier (1532) in the gilded Chapel of St. Wenceslas

Progress was halted abruptly by the troubles of the 15th century, and the cathedral consisted only of an east end until the formation of an 'Association for the Completion of the Cathedral', in 1843. Decades of effort saw the nave, western towers and much else brought to a triumphant conclusion; in 1929, a thousand years after Prince Wenceslas was assassinated, the cathedral was consecrated, dedicated to St. Vitus, commonly regarded as a patron saint of Bohemia.

Cathedral treasures The cathedral is a treasure house of Bohemian history, though the Crown Jewels, its greatest prize, are seldom on display. The spacious interior absorbs the crowds with ease and provides a fitting context for an array of precious objects that range from medieval paintings to modern stained glass.

THE BASICS

www.svatyvit.cz

✚ D6

✉ Pražský hrad

☎ 224 373 368

🕐 Apr–end Oct daily 9–5; Nov–end Mar daily 9–4. Tower: daily 9–4

🍴 Restaurants and cafés in castle

🚃 Tram 22, 23 to Pražský hrad (Prague Castle)

♿ Fair

💲 Free to walk around inside; sights expensive

Loreta

Church exterior (left);
archway (middle);
roof statue (below)

THE BASICS

www.loreta.cz
⊞ B6
✉ Loretánské náměstí
☎ 220 516 740
🕐 Tue–Sun 9–12.15,
1–4.30
🚊 Tram 22, 23 to
Pohořelec
♿ Few
💷 Moderate

HIGHLIGHTS

● The main façade, with
statuary and carillon
● The Santa Casa
● Interior of the Church of
the Nativity
● Diamond monstrance in
the Loretto Treasury
● Cloister painting of
St. Starosta

**A bearded lady, skeletons rattling their
bones to the sound of chiming bells,
severed breasts and a flying house are
not part of a freak show, but instead are
all features of the sumptuous Loretto
Shrine, on Hradčany Hill.**

Counter-Reformation fireworks After
the Battle of the White Mountain in 1620
Protestant austerity, with its repudiation of
images, was replaced by the idolatry of the cult
of the Virgin Mary, dripping with sensuality and
symbolism. Of all the flights of architectural
fantasy that the Roman Catholic Counter-
Reformation perpetrated on Prague, the
Loretto is the most bizarre as well as the most
beautiful, its church and courtyard an area of
cults, miracles and mysteries.

Weird wonders The kernel of the complex is
a Santa Casa, a facsimile of the Virgin Mary's
holy home in Nazareth, supposedly flown by
angels from the Holy Land and deposited at
Loreto in Italy. It is an ornate little Renaissance
pavilion built in 1631 and later given an equally
ornate baroque setting of courtyard, carillon
tower and richly decorated church. Pilgrims
once flocked here in huge numbers to marvel
at the macabre: St. Agatha offering up her
bloody bosom to the angels; the skeletons in
their wax death masks; unhappy St. Starosta,
whose father killed her in a fury after finding
that she'd grown a beard to discourage a
preferred suitor.

Šternberský palác

Who would guess that the little alley beside the Prague archbishop's palace would lead to one of the nation's great art collections? Housed in the grand Šternberg Palace, it dazzles visitors with its old masters.

Ambitious aristocrats After building the Trojský zámek (Troja Château ▷ 98–99) on the edge of Prague, Count Šternberg, one of the city's richest men, needed a town house closer to Prague Castle. The Italian architect Giovanni Alliprandi designed the palace, and work began on the count's Hradčany home in 1698. However, the money ran out before the completion of the main façade. The interior was decorated with fine ceiling and wall paintings. It was a later Šternberg who donated much of the family's great picture collection to the precursor to the National Gallery in the early 19th century, and the nation's finest foreign paintings were housed here from 1821 to 1871. They are once more in this grand setting.

Picture palace Although tucked away behind Hradčanské náměstí, the Šternberg Palace is substantial, arranged around an imposing courtyard, with grand stairways and an oval pavilion facing the garden. The paintings of the National Gallery of European Art could keep an art lover busy for a day, though some star exhibits are no longer on view: A policy of restitution has returned them to the owners from whom they were confiscated by the Communists.

HIGHLIGHTS

● Triptych of the *Adoration of the Magi*, Giertgen tot Sint Jans
● *Adam and Eve*, Cranach
● *Feast of the Rosary*, Dürer
● *Scholar in his Study*, Rembrandt
● *Head of Christ*, El Greco
● Portraits from 2nd-century Egypt
● *Beheading of St. Dorothy*, Hans Baldung Grien
● *Eleonora of Toledo*, Bronzino
● *St. Jerome*, Ribera

HRADČANY

TOP 25

71

Pražský hrad

TOP
25

● Vladislav Hall in Old Royal Palace
● 'Story of the Castle' exhibition
● Golden Lane

● The best time to see the Changing of the Guard at the western entrance is at midday, when there is a more elaborate ceremony, enhanced by a musical accompaniment.
● The most cost-effective way to see the castle and associated attractions (including cathedral, palace and Golden Lane), is to buy a combined entry ticket. Purchase tickets at the Prague Information Centre, in the castle's second and third courtyards.

The thousand windows of Prague Castle gaze over the city. This is the citadel of the Czech nation and it holds its collective memory. It includes palaces, churches, streets, squares and treasures.

Castle denizens At the castle's western gates, blue-uniformed guardsmen stand to attention beneath a pair of battling baroque giants. Beyond, a series of courtyards echo with the tread of countless ghosts: from emperors like Charles IV and Rudolph II to the rulers of modern times.

Exploring the castle The castle offers plenty of attractions. In the Starý královský palác/Old Royal Palace, the gloriously vaulted Vladislavský sál/Vladislav Hall is spacious enough to have

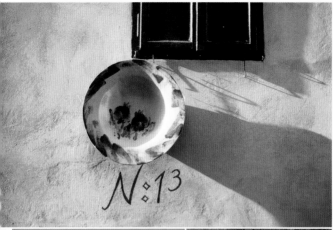

Clockwise from left: a guard in his box at Prague Castle; descending the Zámecké schody (New Castle Steps); detail of No 13 Golden Lane (Zlatá ulička); Golden Lane built into the fortifications of the castle; looking across the river toward Malá Strana and the castle; cobbled Golden Lane

served for tournaments. In 1618, from an adjacent room, the Prague Defenestration took place, when Catholic councillors were thrown out into the moat, though a dungheap broke their fall. Their survival is marked by a monument in the gardens along the southern ramparts. The northern ramparts can be explored, too, and built into their walls are the brightly painted 'alchemists' cottages' of Zlatá ulička/Golden Lane. To immerse yourself in the past of the castle, descend into its labyrinthine substructure, which now houses 'The Story of the Castle', a succession of fascinating, state-of-the-art displays. Children will enjoy the Muzeum hraček/Toy Museum just off Jiřská ulička, the lane leading down to the Černá věž/Black Tower guarding the eastern entrance to the citadel.

THE BASICS

www.hrad.cz
✚ C/D6
✉ Pražský hrad
☎ 224 373 368
🕐 Courtyards and streets: daily until late. Buildings: Apr–end Oct daily 9–5; Nov–end Mar 9–4
🍴 Cafés and restaurants
🚇 Malostranská, then an uphill walk
🚊 Tram 22, 23 to Pražský hrad
♿ Few 💷 Moderate

Strahovský klášter

HIGHLIGHTS

- 17th-century Theological Hall
- 18th-century Philosophical Hall
- Strahovská obrazárna (Strahov Picture Gallery)
- 9th-century Strahov Gospels

TIP

- Strahov has a Cabinet of Curiosities in its lobby, the weird and wonderful objects here matched by the microscopic oddities in the Muzeum Miniatur on the far side of the courtyard.

Baroque spires rising to Heaven, a gilded image of an enemy of the Faith, monks profiting from an enterprise in Hell: The Strahov Monastery seems to encapsulate something of this paradoxical city.

Persuasive priests The Strahov Monastery, a landmark in the cityscape, crowns the steep slope up from Malá Strana. It is a treasure-house of literature, and its ornate library halls, with their splendid frescoes, are among the most magnificent in Europe. As befits a monastery devoted to books, Strahov owed much to its abbots' ways with words. Its 12th-century founder, Abbot Zdík, persuaded Prince Vladislav II to back his project by making flattering comparisons of Prague with the holy city of Jerusalem. Much later, in 1783, Abbot Meyer

From the left: detail of the ceiling fresco depicting the Banquet of King Balthasar, decorating the ceiling of the former abbot's dining room; the exterior of the monastery, with the statue of St. Norbert on the top; the 9th-century Strahov Gospel, with a richly bejewelled cover, in the monastery

exercised equal powers of persuasion on Emperor Joseph II to exempt Strahov from his edict that closed down many of the Habsburg Empire's monasteries. The cleric was so eloquent that Strahov benefited from the misfortune of other institutions: Books from the suppressed monastery at Louka were brought here by the wagonload. A gilded medallion of the emperor over the library entrance may also have helped to persuade Joseph that the Strahov monks deserved special treatment.

Returnees' revenge The monks, of the Premonstratensian Order, were chased out of Strahov by the Communists in 1952, but have come back. The upper floor of the cloisters is a gallery for the art returned to them; a wine cellar is now a restaurant called Peklo (Hell).

THE BASICS

www.
strahovskyklaster.cz
✚ B7
✉ Strahovské nádvoří 1
☎ 233 107 711
🕐 Library halls: daily 9–12, 1–5. Gallery: Tue–Sun 9–12, 12.30–5
🍴 Peklo (Hell) restaurant in monastery cellars
🚃 Tram 22, 23 to Pohořelec
♿ Fair
💰 Moderate

More to See

ARCIBISKUPSKÝ PALÁC (ARCHBISHOP'S PALACE)

The lusciously restored rococo façade hides a sumptuous residence, unfortunately accessible only on special occasions.

➕ C6 ✉ Hradčanské náměstí 16 ⊙ Not normally open to public 🚋 Trams 22, 23 to Pražský hrad

BELVEDÉR

Also known as the Královský letohrádek (Royal Summer Palace), the Belvedere at the eastern end of the Royal Garden was built in the mid-16th century by Ferdinand I for his beloved consort, Queen Anna. With its elegant arcade and its roof in the shape of an upturned boat, it was one of the first buildings in Central Europe to be inspired by the ideas of the Italian Renaissance. It is used for temporary exhibitions. In the middle of the formal garden setting off the Belvedér stands the Singing Fountain, which gets its name from the resonance made by the water falling into its basin.

➕ D6 ✉ Mariánské hradby 52 ☎ 224 372 327 ⊙ Open only for temporary exhibitions 🚋 Tram 22, 23 to Královský letohrádek

ČERNÍNSKÝ PALÁC (ČERNÍN PALACE)

This monstrous mass of masonry, one of the biggest of all Prague's palaces, was begun by Jan Humprecht, Count Czernin, in 1669, bankrupting his family for generations to come. Eventually it became a barracks, then the country's Foreign Ministry. In 1948, after the Communist coup, it was here that another infamous Prague defenestration took place, that of democratic Foreign Minister Jan Masaryk.

➕ B7 ✉ Loretánské náměstí ⊙ Not open to public 🚋 Tram 22, 23 to Pohořelec

KRÁLOVSKÁ ZAHRADA (ROYAL GARDENS)

The trees and lawns of the Royal Gardens stretch out along the

Exterior of the 18th-century Šternberský palác (▷ 71)

The Renaissance façade of Černín Palace, reflected on the roof of a car

plateau on the far side of the Stag Moat defending the northern flank of the Castle. Long ago they housed the imperial zoo, whose denizens included lions, tigers and even a dodo. Europe's first tulips were grown here. Nowadays the gardens offer an escape from the crowds, as well as providing unusual views of the Castle and Cathedral. Apart from the lovely Belvedér (▷ 76), the most fascinating structure in the gardens is the mid-16th-century Míčovna (Ball Game Hall); if you look hard among its sgraffito decoration you can find a hammer and sickle, clandestinely inserted in Communist times.

✚ C/D6 ✉ Královská zahrada ⏰ Apr–end Oct daily 10–6 🚋 Tram 22, 23 to Královský letohrádek or Pražský hrad ♿ Free

NOVÝ SVĚT

A world away from the pomp of Hradčany's palaces, this rustic little quarter is like a piece of countryside left over from the city's expansion.

Basically consisting of a single winding lane, Nový Svět (New World) itself has become a quiet residential enclave and has resisted commercialization. In the past, its picturesque dwellings housed the castle's servants, as well as rather more eminent clients of the royal household such as astronomer Tycho Brahe and mathematician Johannes Kepler.

✚ B/C6 ✉ Nový Svět 🍴 Restaurant at No. 3 🚋 Tram 22, 23 to Brusnice ♿ Few

SCHWARZENBERSKÝ PALÁC (SCHWARZENBERG PALACE)

The city's most imposing Renaissance palace is just outside Prague Castle, its sgraffito-bedecked façade and bristling gables making a noble impression. It now houses the National Gallery's fine collection of baroque and mannerist art.

✚ C6 ✉ Hradčanské náměstí 2 ☎ 233 081 713 ⏰ Closed for reconstruction 🚋 Trams 22, 23 to Pražský hrad

Exterior detail of the delightful Schwarzenberg Palace

Street sign and lamp on Nový Svět

Hradčany to Malá Strana

After exploring the byways of Hradčany, this walk follows an unusual route down to Malá Strana.

DISTANCE: 3km (2 miles) **ALLOW:** 1.5 hours

WALK

1 At the courtyard of Strahovský klašter, turn right down steps, which pass beneath the buildings.

8 Turn right along Tomášská, which brings you into Malostranské náměstí, with its busy tram stop.

HRADČANY

2 Turn right on emerging into the square, take the left fork and turn left downhill to the Loreta. Bear left across the square and walk down the lane of Černínská.

7 The exit from the gardens brings you into Valdštejnské náměstí (Wallenstein Square), dominated by the great palace built by General Wallenstein, now the home of the Senate.

3 This brings you to Nový Svět, where you turn right and walk along the winding cobbled street that brings you eventually into palace-lined Hradčanské náměstí.

6 At the Moravská bašta, marked by a slim column, go down the steps and buy a ticket for the stunning and dramatic Palácové zahrady (Palace Gardens).

4 Enter the castle at the western entrance and walk to the Third Courtyard on the southern side of the cathedral. At the far end of the courtyard descend the stairway, to emerge into the gardens in the southern ramparts.

5 Turn left and walk along the ramparts, enjoying the view down into Malá Strana.

Shopping

GAMBRA

The little Nový Svět gallery has intriguing art objects and books.

➕ B6 ✉ Černínská 5
🚊 Tram 22, 23 to Brusnice; 22, 23 to Pohořelec

HRAČKY

Tiny old-fashioned toy store loaded with low-tech wooden toys, including spinning tops, cars, dragons and animals. Also games, hand-painted dolls, cloth dolls and metal cars all at reasonable prices.

➕ B/C7 ✉ Loretánské náměstí 3 ☎ 603 515 745
🚊 Tram 22, 23 to Pohořelec

MUSEUM SHOP

Unusually tasteful and original souvenirs based on the treasures of the many Prague museums, plus foreign art books not available elsewhere in Prague. An example of other souvenir shops worldwide; where else, for example, could you buy a china mug with such elegant sgraffito patterning?

➕ C6 ✉ Pražský hrad
☎ 224 373 264 🚊 Tram 22, 23 to Pražský hrad

ZLATÁ ULIČKA (GOLDEN LANE)

Even though you have to pay to get in (tickets from the Castle ticket office), picturesque Golden Lane, with its line of quaint and cheerful little cottages, is worth visiting if you are in search of unusual souvenirs. The former homes of goldsmiths, these tiny buildings are now shops selling a variety of items, among them (at No. 23) a fascinating selection of antique prints and maps. You can stop for a coffee or lunch break in this street, too.

➕ D6 ✉ Zlatá ulička, Pražský hrad

HRADČANY

🎁

SHOPPING

Restaurants

PRICES

Prices are approximate, based on a 3-course meal for one person.

£££ over 800Kč
££ 400Kč–800Kč
£ under 400Kč

LOBKOWICZ PALACE CAFÉ (£)

This aristocratic establishment occupies a couple of tastefully decorated rooms in a private palace forming part of the castle complex. It's easily the best place hereabouts for a snack or light meal, especially if you sit out on the balcony overlooking the castle gardens.

✚ D6 ✉ Jiřská 3, Pražský hrad ☎ 602 595 998 🚊 Malostranská, or tram 22, 23 to Pražský hrad

LVÍ DVŮR (££)

In a strategic setting on the northern approach to the castle, the historic 'Lion Court' uses its name to evoke the wild beasts once kept here in the imperial zoo. Meat such as venison features on the menu, though the specialty is a whole suckling pig cooked on a spit.

✚ C6 ✉ U Pražného mostu 6 ☎ 224 372 361 🚊 Tram 22, 23 to Pražský hrad

U ČERNÉHO VOLA (£)

Really more of an old-fashioned pub than a true restaurant, but nevertheless turns out decent traditional dishes at very affordable prices. Great spot to nip in for a quick pint.

✚ B7 ✉ Loretánská náměstí 1 ☎ 220 513 481 🚊 Tram 22, 23 to Pohořelec

U CÍSAŘŮ (££)

This ancient building has an ambience worthy of its name 'At the Emperor's'. The atmospheric, vaulted rooms include arms and armour, aristocratic portraits, and the occasional bearskin. The menu is international and Czech cuisine.

✚ C7 ✉ Loretánská 5 ☎ 220 518 484 🚊 Tram 22, 23 to Pohořelec

U ZLATÉ HRUŠKY (£££)

Serving traditional Bohemian dishes as well as more international fare, the 'Golden Pear' occupies a lovely old baroque residence

BEWARE

Prague waiters have largely overcome a reputation for overcharging. But it makes sense to check your bill carefully before paying. A common (and acceptable) practice is the offer before the meal of tempting hors d'oeuvres. These aren't complimentary, and you will have to pay for them.

on the charming lane of Nový Svět. It also has an attractive garden section.

✚ C7 ✉ Nový Svět 3 ☎ 220 514 778 🚊 Tram 22, 23 to Brusnice

U ZLATÉ STUDNĚ (££–£££)

Pressed up against the southern ramparts of the castle, the restored 'Golden Well' is one of Prague's most prestigious hotels and restaurants. Strictly speaking it is part of Malá Strana, but is included here for its lovely outdoor café reached by going down a few steps from the Castle's south gardens.

✚ D6 ✉ U Zlaté studně 166 ☎ 257 011 213 🚊 Malostranská, or tram 22, 23 to Pražský hrad

VIKÁRKA (££)

The historic quarters once lived in by the cathedral's curates are partly occupied by this reopened restaurant. With its traditional ambience and its interesting take on old Czech dishes, it's perhaps the best place in the Castle precincts to interrupt your sightseeing with a substantial meal.

✚ D6 ✉ Vikářská 39, Pražský hrad ☎ 233 311 962 🚊 Tram 22, 23 to Pražský hrad

Perched below the Castle, Mala Strana (Lesser Town) is Prague's most prefectly preserved historic district, an area of palaces and gardens, now peppered with chic restaurants and smart hotels.

6

7

8

9

10

zám schody   Thunovsk

sv Kajetán † **Nerudova**
        Nerudova   P

                            Chrám sv
                            Mikuláše

sv Karel
Boromejský †   Vlašská   Tržiště

        Vlašská   **Vrtbovská**
                Lobkovický   Schönbornský   **zahrada**
                palác   palác
                                      Panny Marie
                                      Vítězné

    Lobkovická
    zahrada   **MALÁ STRANA**

Strahovská   Hellichova
zahrada
                Petřínská   *Seminářská*
                rozhledna   *zahrada*
    Strahovská   Zrcadlové
                    bludiště
                        ✠ sv Vavřinec

                    Petřín   *Pětřínské sady*
    Olympijská

    Chaloupeckého

                    Kinského zahrada

0   250 m
0   250 yds

B   C   D

Ledeburská
zahrada

**Palácové
zahrady**

Ledeburský
palác

Valdštejnská

Malostranská

Senát

**Valdštejnský
palác**

Letenská

Mánesův most

Klášter
sv Tomáše

Tomášská

Vojanovy
sady

Minist
financí

U lužického semináře

Cihelna

**Franz Kafka
Museum**

**Malostranské
náměstí**

sv Josefa

Josefská

Muzeum

Mišeňská

Malostranské
náměstí

Mostecká

Saská

Lázeňská

Hroznová

Karlův most

Prokopská

**Panny Marie
pod řetězem**

Na rampě

Lichtenštejnský
palác

Karmelitská

Nosticova

Hellichova

Čertovka

KAMPA

Kampa

**Muzeum
hudby**

Tyršovo
muzeum

U sovových mlýnů

**Muzeum
Kampa**

Vltava

Újezd

Všehrdova

sv Jana
na prádle

Malostranské nábřeží

Říční

Újezd

Vítězná

most Legií

Janáčkovo nábřeží

Plaská

Zborovská

Mělnická

Újezd

E

F

Chrám sv Mikuláše

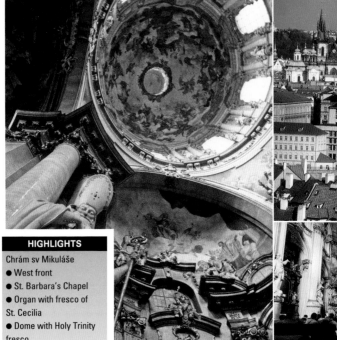

HIGHLIGHTS

Chrám sv Mikuláše
● West front
● St. Barbara's Chapel
● Organ with fresco of St. Cecilia
● Dome with Holy Trinity fresco
● Huge sculptures of four Church Fathers
● Trompe-l'oeil ceiling fresco by Kracker

TIP

● The 215 steps of the bell tower of St. Nicholas's Church (entrance on south side of the building) are well worth climbing; from the top there are fantastic views, including close-ups of the church's dome and statuary as well as of the whole of Malá Strana and the city beyond.

As you walk around the base of the lofty St. Nicholas's Church, you feel the power of the Catholic Counter-Reformation expressed in one of the most beautiful baroque buildings of Central Europe.

Counter-Reformation citadel When the Jesuits came to Prague following the route of the Protestants at the Battle of the White Mountain, the existing little 13th-century church at the middle of Malostranské náměstí (Malá Strana Square) was far too modest for their aspirations. The new St. Nicholas's Church was eventually completed in the 18th century and, with its lofty walls and high dome and bell tower, became one of the dominant features of the city. The Jesuits intended their church to impress, but not through size alone.

Clockwise from left: the frescoes decorating the walls and cupola; view from the church across the Vltava river to the towers of Týn Church, Powder Gate and St. Nicholas; the curving façade and green copper dome and tower of the church; the magnificent interior

They employed the finest architects of the day (the Dientzenhofers, father and son, plus Anselmo Lurago), along with talented interior designers. Inside, no effort was spared to enthral via the dynamic play of space, statuary and painting, a fantastically decorated pulpit and a 2,500-pipe organ (played by Mozart on several occasions). Today, the church still frequently holds classical music concerts.

Princely palaces and humbler households In front of the huge church swirls the life of Malá Strana—locals waiting for the trams mixing with visitors following the Royal Way up to Hradčany. Malostranské náměstí is lined with a fascinating mixture of ancient town houses and grand palaces, while attached to St. Nicholas's is the Jesuits's college, now part of the university.

THE BASICS

www.psalterium.cz
✚ D7
✉ Malostranské náměstí
☎ 257 534 215
🕐 Mar–end Oct daily 9–5; Nov–end Mar daily 9–4. Tower: Apr–early Nov daily 10–5
🍴 Restaurants and cafés in square
Ⓜ Malostranská
🚊 Tram 12, 20, 22, 23 to Malostranské náměstí
♿ Few 💷 Inexpensive; concerts expensive

Malostranské náměstí

TOP 25

Bar sign (left);
Lobkovický palác
(German embassy,
middle); aerial view

THE BASICS

+ D7
⊠ Malostranské náměstí
⬛ Tram 12, 20, 22, 23 to Malostranské náměstí

TIP

● The square offers exciting possibilities for taking photographs at all times of day and night. Floodlighting transforms the great presence of the Church of St. Nicholas, especially when framed by the square's arcades.

Overlooked by the city's greatest baroque church Chrám sv Mikuláše (Church of St. Nicholas), Malá Strana Square is the hub of the Lesser Town and a focal point on the route between the Old Town and the castle.

A place to relax There's plenty to see and explore in and around the square and nearby streets and lanes. It's here in the heart of Malá Strana (Lesser Town) that most visitors pause before tackling the steep climb up to the Castle, not least because of the temptation offered by the bars, cafés and restaurants.

The buildings St. Nicholas divides the sloping square into an upper and a lower half, each lined by the palaces and patrician houses so characteristic of this part of town. Some are very old, but most were rebuilt or given new façades in baroque style in the late 17th and 18th centuries. The grandest of the aristocratic edifices is the Lichtenštejnský palác (Lichtenstein Palace), which takes up the whole of the western side of the square. Built on the orders of Karl von Lichtenstein (1569–1627), it now houses the music faculty of the university. Take time to admire the broad arcades of the burgher's houses along the south of the square, and peer into the entrance of No. 1/272, a fine example of an old-fashioned Prague *pavlač* (galleried court-yard); it has the enchanting name of U petržílka (Parsley House).

View to Vltava from the Petřín Tower (below); the Mirror Maze on the hill

Petřín

When the crowds on Charles Bridge become too much, there's always the glorious green of Petřín Hill, its orchards and woodlands a cool retreat from the middle of the city—and a real breath of the countryside in the metropolis.

A train with a view In 1891, for the city's great Jubilee Expo that celebrated the achievements of the Czech provinces when they still formed part of the Austrian Empire, the city leaders provided a jolly little funicular railway (the 'Lanovka') to the top of Petřín Hill. Now restored, it once again carries passengers effortlessly up the steep slope. At the top there's a whole array of attractions, including the Rozhledna ('Lookout'), the little brother of the Eiffel Tower, also built in 1891. Its 299 steps lead to a viewing platform offering a fantastic panorama over the city. Next to the tower, the old-fashioned Mirror Maze (Bludiště) continues to work its hilarious magic. In the same building is an equally old-fashioned but effective diorama depicting an historic battle on Charles Bridge.

Country matters With its woods and orchards (splendid in spring), Petřín provides a welcome counterpoint to the busy castle area. Once there were vineyards on the hill, but these didn't survive the Thirty Years' War in the 17th century. They were replaced by the superb gardens that link the palaces of Malá Strana to the surrounding hillside parklands.

THE BASICS

➕ C/D 7–8
🌐 Rozhledna, Mirror Maze: May–end Sep daily 10–10; Oct–end Apr daily 10–6
🍽 Restaurant and café
🚋 Funicular railway, from Újezd in Malá Strana
🚃 Tram 22, 23 to Pohořelec then walk
♿ Few
💷 Rozhledna, Mirror Maze: inexpensive

HIGHLIGHTS

● Rozhledna viewing tower
● 4th-century Hunger Wall
● Mirror Maze (Bludiště)
● Charles Bridge Battle diorama

MALÁ STRANA

★

TOP 25

Valdštejnský palác

Statues in the formal garden (left); relief work on a heavy brass palace door

HIGHLIGHTS

● Sala Terrena
● Garden sculptures (copies of originals by de Vries)
● Grotesquery and aviary in garden

Think of Wallenstein Palace—Prague's biggest palace—as an awful warning to eschew the excessive ambition of its builder, Albrecht von Wallenstein, whose desire for power led to his assassination.

Greedy generalissimo Wallenstein's huge late Renaissance/early baroque palace crouches at the foot of Prague Castle as if waiting greedily to gobble it up. A whole city block was demolished to make way for the complex of five courtyards, a barracks, a riding school and a superb garden that were intended to reflect Wallenstein's wealth and status. Wallenstein (Valdštejn in Czech) turned the troubled early 17th century to his advantage. Having wormed his way into the emperor's good graces, he became governor of Prague, then Duke of Friedland. He married for money (twice), and great tracts of land (even towns) fell into his hands following the Battle of the White Mountain in 1620. His fortune grew more as he quartermastered the imperial armies as well as leading them. Rightly suspicious of his subject's intentions, the emperor had him killed.

The general's garden The great hall of the palace can be seen only on special occasions, as the Czech Senate now occupies the building. More freely accessible, the formal garden is dominated by the superb Sala Terrena loggia, fashioned on those in Italy, and has convincing copies of the statues stolen by Swedish soldiers during the Thirty Years' War.

More to See

FRANZ KAFKA MUSEUM

www.kafkamuseum.cz

For all those who feel they should know more about the famous writer, this innovative exhibition is the answer. Unusual souvenir shop.

⊞ E7 ☒ Cihelná 2B ☎ 257 535 507 ◎ Daily 10–6 ⓠ Malostranská ⬛ Moderate

MUZEUM HUDBY

www.nm.cz

The National Museum of Music, in the stimulating setting of a Malá Strana church, exhibits instruments and memorabilia. After costly conversion, the nave now functions as a fine concert hall, overlooked by several floors of side galleries in which the collections are expertly displayed. Every conceivable type of instrument is on show, from violins once owned by virtuosos to some extremely odd-looking bagpipes, a Czech specialty. Even odder are the bulbous brass instruments arranged in artful patterns in their showcases.

⊞ D7 ☒ Karmelitská 2/4 ☎ 257 257 777 ◎ Wed–Mon 10–6 ⬛ Moderate 🚋 Tram 12, 20, 22, 23 to Hellichová

MUZEUM KAMPA

www.museumkampa.cz

This superb conversion of an historic mill houses an important collection of modern Czech art.

⊞ E8 ☒ U Sovových mlýnů 2 ☎ 257 286 147 ◎ Daily 10–6 🍴 Riverside restaurant and café 🚋 Trams 12, 20, 22, 23 to Hellichova ⬛ Moderate

NERUDOVA

One of Prague's loveliest streets, Nerudova forms part of the Royal Route, rising steeply from Malá Strana Square toward the castle. The climb reveals one delight after another: baroque town houses with elaborate house signs proclaiming their names ('The Three Little Fiddles', 'The Golden Key'), stately palaces with portals guarded by pairs of eagles or muscular moors. House No. 47 ('The Two Suns) was the home of the 19th-century writer Jan Neruda, who depicted the

Baroque and Renaissance buildings lining Nerudova

doings of the denizens of Malá Strana with a Dickensian pen.

🏠 C/D7 ✉ Nerudova 201
🍴 Restaurants and cafés 🚊 Trams 12, 20, 22, 23 to Malostranské náměstí ♿ Few

PALÁCOVÉ ZAHRADY (PALACE GARDENS)

This glorious group of terraced (formerly private) gardens of artistocratic families, clings to the near-vertical slope dropping from the castle ramparts to the palaces lining Valdštejnská street. Apart from their intrinsic attractiveness, they form an intriguing alternative route to and from the Hradčany heights (though only in season).

🏠 D6 ✉ Valdštejnské náměstí 3 (also enter through Valdštejnské ul. 12) ☎ 257 010 401 🕐 Apr–end Oct daily 10–8
💷 Moderate 🚇 Malostranská 🚊 Tram 12, 20, 22, 23 to Malostranské náměstí

PANNY MARIE VÍTĚZNÉ

www.pragjesu.info
The Church of Our Lady of Victory welcomes pilgrims from all over the world, who come to venerate the wax figurine known as the Bambino di Praga. Originally dedicated to the Holy Trinity, the church was given its present name following the 1620 Battle of the White Mountain, when it was handed over to the Spanish Carmelite order. In 1628 the church was given the little figure of the infant Jesus, which became the focus of a widespread cult.

🏠 D7 ✉ Karmelitská 9 ☎ 257 533 646
🕐 Church: Mon–Sat 8.30–6.30, Sun 9.30–8 (hours may vary). Museum: Mon–Sat 10–5.30, Sun 1–5 💷 Free
🚊 Tram 12, 20, 22, 23 to Hellichova or Malostranské náměstí

VRTBOVSKÁ ZAHRADA (VRTBA GARDEN)

www.vrtbovska.cz
Prague's finest individual baroque garden has sculptures and a view over Malá Strana.

🏠 D7 ✉ Karmelitská 25 ☎ 257 531 480
🕐 Apr–end Oct daily 10–6 🚊 Tram 12, 20, 22, 23 to Malostranské náměstí
💷 Inexpensive

Trees frame the Church of Our Lady of Victory

The slender green-copper spire of the Church of St. Thomas

Malá Strana

This walk allows you to discover some of the less frequented parts of Prague's best-preserved historic district.

DISTANCE: 3.5km (2 miles) **ALLOW:** 2 hours

START

MALOSTRANSKÁ METRO
➕ E6 🚇 Malostranská

END

MALOSTRANSKÉ NÁMĚSTÍ
➕ D7 🚋 Tram 12, 20, 22, 23

MALÁ STRANA

WALK

① From the station find your way to the upstream approach to Mánes Bridge. Turn right down steps into the little riverside park from where there are unusual Old Town views.

② At the far end of the park, turn left into Cihelná. The street is named after an old brickworks, now a restaurant. The Kafka Museum is in its courtyard.

③ Continue in the same direction, bearing left over Čertovka (Devil's Brook), and pass beneath one of the arches of the Charles Bridge.

④ You are now in Kampa Island. At the start of parkland go right to recross Čertovka. Bear right at the end of the park and follow a narrow street to Maltézské náměstí (Maltese Square).

⑧ Nerudova leads down into upper Malostranské náměstí. The busy tram stop is in the lower part of the square.

⑦ Go up little Šporkova opposite the German Emabssy and follow it round, turning left up steps that bring you onto one of Prague's loveliest streets, Nerudova. Turn right and walk slowly downhill past baroque and rococo town houses.

⑥ Cross the road and walk up Tržiště. Continue uphill, bearing left into Vlašská. The magnificent Lobkovický palác houses the German Embassy.

⑤ Walk across and head left into Prokopsá at the far end, and turn right along busy Karmelistská.

Shopping

AHASVER ANTIQUES

An unusual little establishment with an intriguing line in vintage apparel, lace, linen and accessories.

⊕ D7 ⊠ Prokopská 3 ☎ 257 531 404 ⏲ Tue–Sun 11–6 🚊 Tram 12, 20, 22, 23 to Hellichova or Malostranské náměstí

KOŽEŠINY KUBÍN

A modest alternative to the grandiose Liska shop in the Old Town, this is a privately run little fur and leather shop.

⊕ D8 ⊠ Vítězná 12 ☎ 257 323 600 ⏲ Mon–Fri 9–6, Sat 9–1 🚇 Újezd

OBCHOD S LOUTKAMI

Head here when not just any marionette will do. Some of the finest handmade puppets available in Prague. Some of the individual designs can be expensive but others are reasonably priced. Supplied by more than 30 different craftspeople.

⊕ D7 ⊠ Nerudova 51 ☎ 257 533 035 ⏲ Daily 10–6 🚊 Tram 12, 20, 22, 23 to Malostranské náměstí

PAVLA A OLGA

Original and innovative fashion from acclaimed fashion designers.

⊕ C7 ⊠ Vlašská 13 ☎ 728 939 872 ⏲ PM only 🚊 Tram 12, 20, 22, 23 to Malostranské náměstí

U ZLATÉ ČÍŠE

As well as secondhand books, this treasure cave of an antiquarian bookshop has a changing stock of old posters, postcards, prints and banknotes, and even a limited number of miniature versions of the distinctive Prague street signs and house numbers.

⊕ D7 ⊠ Nerudova 16 ☎ 257 531 393 ⏲ Daily 10–6 🚊 Tram 12, 20, 22, 23 to Malostranské náměstí

Entertainment and Nightlife

CHRÁM SV MIKULÁŠE

The organ that Mozart played in Prague's greatest baroque church still accompanies choral concerts.

⊕ D7 ⊠ Malostranské náměstí 25 ☎ 257 534 215 🚊 Tram 12, 20, 22, 23 to Malostranské náměstí

LICHTENŠTEJNSKÝ PALÁC

The setting for symphonic and other performances. Home of the Prague Music Academy where students

perform regularly.
⊕ D7 ⊠ Malostranské náměstí 13 ☎ 257 534 206 🚊 Tram 12, 20, 22, 23 to Malostranské náměstí

PRAGUE PUPPETS

Puppetry has a long tradition in the Czech lands, and puppets are certainly not just for children. Collectors pay good money for hand-carved marionettes, and there are several venues that bring these dolls to life. Among the most-loved figures are those of the serio-comic duo of Speibl (father) and son Hurvínek.

U MALÉHO GLENA

Little Glenn's is named after its genial owner, who plays recorded jazz in the upstairs bar and the real thing—alternating with pop or rock—in the basement. Sunday night jam sessions bring out some of Prague's best jazz musicians.

⊕ D7 ⊠ Karmelitská 23 ☎ 257 531 717 🚊 Tram 12, 20, 22, 23 to Malostranské náměstí

Restaurants

PRICES

Prices are approximate, based on a 3-course meal for one person.

£££	over 800Kč
££	400Kč–800Kč
£	under 400Kč

ALCHYMIST (£££)

Opened in 2004, and recently renovated, with an intimate but sumptuous interior to complement its inventive cuisine.
🚇 D7 ✉ Hellichova 4 ☎ 257 312 518 🚊 Tram 12, 20, 22, 23 to Hellichova

BAR BAR (£)

Not a bar in the American or Western European sense, rather a relaxed student pub/café with good value entrées like tasty crêpes, sandwiches and salads. Large, but warm dining room. Friendly staff.
🚇 D8 ✉ Všehrdova 17 ☎ 257 312 246 🚇 Malostranská 🚊 Tram 6, 12, 20, 22, 23 to Újezd

BOHEMIA BAGEL (£)

A long-established hangout for North American expats and visitors, the Bagel serves classic breakfasts, hearty soups and well-filled rolls, as well as abundant coffee.
🚇 D7 ✉ Lázenská 19 ☎ 257 218 192 🚇 Tram 12, 20, 22, 23 to Malostranské náměstí

CAFÉ DE PARIS (££)

Excellent steaks and French-inspired cooking on one of Malá Strana's quietest and most romantic corners. The wine selection is one of the best in the local district, with plenty of affordable reds and whites—both Czech and French.
🚇 D7 ✉ Maltese náměstí 4 ☎ 603 160 718 🚇 Malostranská 🚊 Tram 12, 20, 22, 23 to Malostranské náměstí

CAFÉ SAVOY (££)

Kafka hung out here when it was a humble café. Now more classy, it's gaining a reputation for its French-inspired cuisine and fresh seafood.
🚇 D8 ✉ Vítězná 5 ☎ 257 311 562 🚊 Tram 6, 9, 22, 23 to Újezd

DUMPLINGS

Bohemian dumplings (*knedlíky*) are made from bread, potato dough, flour or soft curd. They are needed as accompaniments to meat dishes to soak up the grease and beer. However, they also come in more sophisticated guises, such as fruit dumplings. The most mouth-watering of these are filled with strawberries, plums, apricots or sour cherries and have a butter and icing topping.

ČERNÝ OREL (£)

An enclosed courtyard and rustic interior lend this 18th-century inn the feeling of being removed from the bustling city streets and a place to chill out.
🚇 E7 ✉ U Lužického semináře 40 ☎ 257 531 738 🚇 Malostranská

CODA (£££)

Irresistible international dishes served in the stunning ambience of the covered courtyard of the Aria Hotel, or on a rooftop terrace in summer.
🚇 D7 ✉ Tržiště 9 ☎ 225 334 761 🚇 Tram 12, 20, 22, 23 to Malostranské náměstí

COWBOYS (££–£££)

This popular steak restaurant, managed by the same group that runs pricier Kampa Park (▷ 94), is recommendable chiefly for its location just below Prague Castle. It's the best restaurant within easy walking distance of the castle compound. Excellent imported steaks but also lighter and cheaper fare—like sandwiches and salads —served at lunch. In nice weather, request a table on the rooftop terrace.
🚇 C7 ✉ Nerudova 40 ☎ 296 826 107 🚇 Malostranská 🚊 Tram 12, 20, 22, 23 to Malostranské náměstí (plus long walk uphill)

DAVID (£££)

An intimate setting and faultless food, including melt-in-the-mouth lamb, a house specialty.

🚇 D7 ✉ Tržiště 21 ☎ 257 533 109 🚊 Tram 12, 20, 22, 23 to Malostranské náměstí

GITANES (£)

This intimate little restaurant transports you deep into the Balkans, with fiery food washed down with a selection of Mediterranean wines.

🚇 D7 ✉ Tržiště 7 ☎ 257 530 163 🚊 Tram 12, 20, 22, 23 to Malostranské náměstí

HERGETOVA CIHELNA (£££)

Stylishly converted historic brickworks with an intriguing contemporary interior and riverside terrace. Equally stylish, contemporary fare.

🚇 E7 ✉ Cihelná 2b ☎ 296 826 103 🚇 Malostranská

HUNGARIAN GROTTO (££)

For a change from Czech cuisine, descend into the brick vaults of this historic establishment, where spicy Magyar dishes are served with good wines from the Hungarian plains and the shores of Lake Balaton.

🚇 D6 ✉ Tomášská 12 ☎ 257 220 370 🚊 Tram 12, 20, 22, 23 to Malostranské náměstí

KAMPA PARK (£££)

The place to come for celebrity spotting in a lovely riverside setting.

🚇 E7 ✉ Na Kampě 8b ☎ 296 826 112 🚇 Malostranská 🚊 Tram 12, 22, 23 to Malostranské náměstí

PÁLFFY PALÁC (£££)

Offering serious cuisine in an elegant and unforgettable 19th-century setting this place has been popular for those in the know for years.

🚇 D6 ✉ Valdštejnská 14 ☎ 257 530 522 🚇 Malostranská

PETŘINSKÉ TERASY (££)

Enjoy well-prepared Czech specialties on the terrace or in the winter garden. Great views.

🚇 C8 ✉ Semínářská zahrada 13 ☎ 257 320 688

FAST FOOD

Western fast food is now available in many places, but better by far (and much cheaper) for a quick snack are the local *obložené chlebíčky* (open-faced sandwiches). Each of these is like a miniature meal, perhaps consisting of a sliver or two of ham or salami and a slice of hard-boiled egg, the whole garnished with mayonnaise and topped with pieces of pickle and red pepper.

🚊 Tram 12, 20, 22, 23 to Hellichova, then walk or take funicular uphill one stop

SOVOVY MLÝNY (££)

The restaurant attached to the modern art gallery in the beautifully restored 'Sova's Mill' offers innovative interpretations of traditional Bohemian dishes such as rabbit and goose. Riverside terrace.

🚇 E8 ✉ U Sovových Mlýnů, Kampa Island ☎ 257 535 900 🚊 Tram 12, 20, 22, 23 to Hellichova

U KOCOURA (£)

The famous old Tomcat, known better for its beer than the food, is a welcome sight on the hard trek up from Malá Strana to Prague Castle. The savoury crêpes are good value. Good place to people-watch as it is popular with the locals as well as tourists.

🚇 D7 ✉ Nerudova 2 ☎ 257 530 107 🚊 Tram 12, 20, 22, 23 to Malostranské náměstí

U MODRÉ KACHNIČKY (££–£££)

In its cozy side-street location the 'Blue Duckling' continues to serve delicious variations on venerable Czech dishes.

🚇 D7 ✉ Nebovidská 6 ☎ 257 320 308 🚊 Tram 12, 20, 22, 23 to Hellichova

Prague's suburbs and outer districts have much to offer. As well as musical shrines to Mozart and Dvořak there are historic buildings like Trojský zámek. The young-at-heart will enjoy the zoo.

TROJA

V HOLEŠOVIČKÁCH

Letecké muzeum

VYCHOVATELNA

LIBEŇ

Thomayerovy sady

Stromovka

HOLEŠOVICE

Veletržní palác

LETNÁ

Národní technické muzeum

Ostrov Štvanice

Vltava

KARLÍN

sady

ROHANSKÉ NÁBŘEŽÍ

Kaizlovy sady

JOSEFOV

PRAGUE

STARÉ MĚSTO

Vrchlického sady

Vrch Vítkov

Národní památník

ŽIŽKOV

Riegrovy sady

Olšanské hřbitovy

VINOHRADY

Chrám Nejsvětějšího Srdce Páně

VINOHRADSKA

ŽITNÁ

Sady Svat Čecha

NOVÉ MĚSTO

Bezručovy sady

RUSKÁ

Heroldovy sady

Havlíčkovy sady

VRŠOVICKÁ

Folimanka

VYŠEHRAD

Vyšehradské sady

NUSELSKÁ

Botič

NA BOHDALCI

NUSLE

TYRŠŮV VRCH

Veslařský ostrov

PANKRÁC

PODOLÍ

Park Družby

MICHLE

DVORCE

KAČEROV

JEREMENKOVA

Trojský zámek

HIGHLIGHTS

● Garden approach on river side of château
● South staircase and terrace with battling Titans
● Grand Hall paintings

TIP

● A good idea is to combine a trip to Troja Château with a visit to Prague Zoo, badly hit by the great flood of 2002 but back in full working order, with a whole host of improvements.

Out here you catch a glimpse of how delightful Prague's countryside must have been three centuries ago, with vine-clad slopes, trees in abundance and the resplendent Troja Château among the allées and parterres.

Prague's Versailles This extravagant baroque palace was built not by the monarch, but by the second richest man in Prague, Count Wenceslas Adelbert Šternberg. The Šternbergs profited from the Thirty Years War, and at the end of the 17th century were in a position to commission Jean-Baptiste Mathey to design a country house along the lines of the contemporary châteaux of the architect's native France. The south-facing site by the river, orientated directly on St. Vitus's Cathedral and Prague

Clockwise from the left: the double staircase leading to the Troja Château; detail of relief decoration on a massive urn crowning a wall in the grounds of the château; wrought-iron gates at the entrance; the red-and-white façade of Troja château; the statue of a mermaid rising from the ornamental pond

Castle on the far side of the Royal Hunting Grounds, now Stromovka Park, was ideal for Šternberg, and it allowed him to offer the monarch the right kind of hospitality following a day's hunting.

Ornamental extravagance The palace's proportions are grandiose, and its painted interiors go over the top in paying homage to the country's Habsburg rulers. And over the top, too, goes a turbaned Turk as he topples, in stunning trompe l'oeil, from the mock battlements in the grand hall. Troja was acquired by the state in the 1920s, but restored only in the late 1980s (some think excessively). It contains part of Prague's collection of 19th-century paintings, few of which can compete with the flamboyance of their setting.

THE BASICS

www.
citygalleryprague.cz
⊞ E1
⊠ U Trojského zámku 1, Troja
☎ 283 851 614
🕐 Tue–Thu, Sun 10–6, Fri 1–7, Sat 10–7
🍴 Restaurant
🚇 Nádraží Holešovice, then bus 112 to Zoologická zahrada
🚊 Trams 5, 12, 17 to Výstaviště, then walk across Stromovka Park and Císařský ostrov (Imperial Island) toward zoo
🚢 PPS boat from Palackého most, Nové Město
♿ Few 💷 Moderate

Veletržní palác

HIGHLIGHTS

- *Winter Evening in Town*, Jakub Schikaneder
- *Reader of Dostoyevsky*, Emil Filla
- *Serie C VI*, František Kupka
- *Melancholy*, Jan Zrzavý
- *Sailor*, Karel Dvořak

TIP

- Trying to see all the works on display in the Trade Fair Palace in one go is likely to lead to visual indigestion. Since tickets are available separately for the individual floors of the gallery, decide on your priorities and plan accordingly. If time is short, you might like to concentrate on the remarkable early-20th-century Czech art on the third floor.

'A truly great experience was a tour of the Prague Trade Fair Building. The first impression...is breathtaking'. So enthused architect Le Corbusier in 1928, shortly after this structure, now the Museum of Modern Art, was completed.

Trailblazer The great master builder and design pioneer Le Corbusier was vexed to find that his Czech colleagues had got in first in completing what is one of the key buildings in the evolution of 20th-century design, a secular, modern-day cathedral constructed in concrete, steel and glass. Set in the suburb of Holešovice, the palace was intended to be a showpiece for the products of Czechoslovakia. However, trade fairs moved away from Prague to Brno, and for many years the great building

Clockwise from left: the exterior of Veletržní palác; the gallery displaying Czech art 1930–2000; penny farthing bicycle with Contemplation (1893) *by Jakub Schikaneder in background;* Motorcyclist (sunbeam), *1924, by Otakar Svec; 1960s Skoda convertible display*

languished in neglect and obscurity, its originality forgotten as its architectural innovations became the norm throughout the world.

Disguised blessing After fire gutted the palace in 1974, it was decided to use its elegant spaces to display the National Gallery's modern art treasures, which had previously been without a proper home. The restoration took around 20 years. Now the engrossing Czech 19th-century collection leads the way to the amazing achievements of Czech artists in the early part of the 20th century. The museum also shows works by French Impressionists and other modern foreign paintings, and promotes contemporary arts of all types, staging the kind of major international art shows of which the Czechs were so long deprived.

THE BASICS

www.ngprague.cz

✚ H4

✉ Dukelských hrdinů 47, Holešovice

☎ 224 301 111

🕐 Tue–Sun 10–6

🍴 Café

🚇 Vltavská

🚊 Tram 5, 12, 14, 17 to Veletržní

♿ Good

💰 Moderate (free first Wed of month from 3pm)

Národní technické muzeum

An early car (left); a guided tour viewing some of the exhibits

HIGHLIGHTS

● 1928 Škoda fire engine
● Laurin and Klement soft-top roadster
● President Masaryk's V-12 Tatra
● Soviet ZIS 110B limousine
● Express locomotive 375-007 of 1911
● Imperial family's railway dining car of 1891
● Bleriot XI Kašpar monoplane
● Sokol monoplane

Did you know that Czechoslovakia had one of the world's biggest auto industries and that Škoda cars are legendary for their reliability? That a horse-drawn railway once linked Bohemia with Austria? That a Czecho-slovak fleet once sailed the oceans?

Past glories The answer to all these questions will be 'yes', after you've visited the wonderful National Technical Museum, off the beaten track on the edge of Letenské sady (Letná Plain). The museum's rich and varied contents celebrate the long-standing technological prowess of inventive and hard-working Czechs. The Czech provinces were the industrial power-house of the Austro-Hungarian Empire, their steel works and coal mines providing the foundation for excellence in engineering, from the production of weapons to locomotive man-ufacture. Later, between the two world wars, independent Czechoslovakia's light industries led the world in innovation and quality.

Trains and boats and planes The museum's collection of technological objects is displayed to spectacular effect in the vast glass-roofed and galleried main hall, where balloons and biplanes hang in space above ranks of sinister-looking streamlined limousines and powerful steam engines. Deep underground there's a mock-up of a coal mine, and other sections tell you all you ever wanted to know about time, sound, geodesy, photography and astronomy.

More to See

BERTRAMKA

This villa was the rural retreat of the Dušeks, Mozart's closest friends in Prague, and it was here that he dashed off the final lines of *Don Giovanni* before conducting its premiere in the Estates Theatre. As well as Mozart memorabilia, on summer evenings, concerts take place in the parklike grounds.

🔲 C11 ✉ Mozartova 169, Smíchov ☎ 257 317 465 🕐 Daily 9–6 🚋 Tram 4, 6, 9, 12, 14 to Bertramka 💵 Inexpensive

BŘEVNOSKÝ KLÁŠTER

The 1,000-year-old Benedictine monastery of Břevnov still has a rustic atmosphere. Its baroque buildings are the work of the Dientzenhofers, and include one of their grandest churches, and an array of other edifices.

🔲 Off map A7 ✉ Markétská 1/28, Břevnov, Prague 6 ☎ 220 406 111 🕐 Apr–end Oct Sat, Sun 10, 2, 4; Nov–end Mar Sat, Sun 10, 2; guided tours only (in Czech) 💵 Inexpensive 🚋 Tram 15, 22, 25 to Břevnovský klášter

CHRÁM NEJSVĚTĚJŠÍHO SRDCE PÁNĚ

Completed in 1932 in Vinohrady, the early modern Sacred Heart church is the masterwork of the Slovene Josip Plečnik, the architect employed in the interwar years to convert Prague Castle into a fitting symbol of the newly created democratic state of Czechoslovakia.

🔲 Off map J9 ✉ Náměstí Jiřího z Poděbrad 19, Vinohrady ☎ 222 727 713 🕐 30 min before and 1 hour after services. Sun 9, 11, 6; Mon–Sat 8–6 🚇 Jiřího z Poděbrad

LETECKÉ MUZEUM

This has one of Europe's largest collections of historic aircraft. Interwar machines demonstrate the energy of the Czechoslovak aircraft industry then. But the stars of the show are the World War II aircraft.

🔲 Off map J1 ✉ Mladoboleslavská 902, Kbely ☎ 973 207 500 🕐 Apr–end Oct Tue–Sun 9.30–6 🚇 Českomoravská, then bus 110, 185, 259, 280 to Letecké Muzeum 💵 Free

The striking structure of the Sacred Heart Church

The interior vaults of the Benedictine Monastery of Břevnov

MÜLLEROVA VILA

www.mullerovavila.cz

The villa, built for the Müller family in 1930, is a key building in the evolution of Functionalist architecture. Its designer was the Viennese architect Adolf Loos (1870–1933). The exterior is severe, but the spatial austerity of the interior is relieved by the use of precious materials.

➕ A6 ✉ Nad Hradním vodojemem 14, Střešovice, Prague 6 ☎ 224 312 012 🕐 Guided tours Tue, Thu, Sat, Sun at 9, 11, 1, 3, 5. Tours must be booked ahead 👋 Expensive 🚇 Hradčanská, then tram 🚃 Tram 1, 2, 18 to Ořechovka

NÁRODNÍ PAMÁTNÍK (NATIONAL MEMORIAL)

Built to commemorate the Czechoslovak legions that fought on the Allied side in World War I, this great slab of a building overlooking the city features a huge equestrian statue of the Hussite, Jan Žižka.

➕ Off map J7 ✉ U Památníku 1900 ☎ 222 781 676 🕐 Due to reopen as a museum after construction work in 2009 or 2010 🚌 Bus 133, 207 to U Památníku and steep uphill walk

VÝSTAVIŠTĚ PRAHA

The extensive art nouveau Exhibition Grounds offer an array of attractions, including a fun fair, performance spaces, a lapidarium and a fine fountain. Nearby is the Planetarium.

➕ G/H3 ✉ U Výstaviště, Holešovice ☎ 220 103 111 🕐 Tue–Fri from 2pm, Sat, Sun from 10am (evening opening for performances) 🍴 Cafés and restaurants 🚃 Tram 5, 12, 14, 17 to Výstaviště 👋 Inexpensive

ZBRASLAV

Visitors come here to see the Zbraslavský zámek, the baroque palace, which is home to the National Gallery's collections of Oriental art and objects.

➕ Off map E12 ✉ Bartoňova 2, Zbraslav, Prague 5 ☎ 257 921 638 🕐 Tue–Sun 10–6 👋 Inexpensive 🚌 Bus 129, 241, 243, 255, 314, 318, 390 from Smíchovské nádraží metro station to Zbraslavské náměstí (14min)

Tomb guardians, Western Jin dynasty, 300BC, in the Zbraslavský zámek in the town of Zbraslav

Prumyslový palác in Výstaviště (Exhibition Park)

Excursions

HRAD KARLŠTEJN (KARLŠTEJN CASTLE)

This mighty fortress, one of the great sights of Bohemia, towers above the glorious woodlands of the gorge of the River Berounka. The castle was started in 1348 by the Emperor Charles IV who conceived it as a sort of sacred bunker, a repository for the Crown Jewels and his collection of holy relics. Book tours in advance.

THE BASICS

www.hradkarlstejn.cz
Distance: 5km (21 miles)
Journey Time: 40 min
☎ Tours: 274 008 154; castle 311 681 617
🚃 Prague–Smíchov to Karlštejn

ZÁMEK KONOPIŠTĚ (KONOPIŠTĚ CASTLE)

Konopiště Castle's round towers rise in romantic fashion above the surrounding woodlands. The palace's origins date to the 14th century, but it owes its present appearance largely to Archduke Franz Ferdinand, heir to the Habsburg throne, who filled it with fine furniture, a weapons collection and trophies of the countless wild creatures he slaughtered. The archduke met his own violent end when he was cut down by an assassin's bullet in Sarajevo, triggering the start of World War I.

THE BASICS

www.zamek-konopiste.cz
Distance: 43km (26 miles)
Journey Time: 45 min by car; 1 hour by train then short trip by local bus or taxi
☎ 317 721 336
🕐 Apr–end Oct Tue–Sun 10–1, 1.30–4
🚃 Hlavní nádraží to Benešov then bus or taxi

KUTNA HORA

One of Bohemia's best-preserved old towns has abundant relics from the glory days when it was a great silver mining hub. A stroll around the streets leads past many minor treasures, such as the Gothic Kamenný dům (Stone House) and the venerable 12-sided public fountain. The town's finest monument is the great Chrám svaté Barbory (St. Barbara's Church), a cathedral-size structure, one of Europe's most extraordinary achievements of late Gothic architecture. In the suburb of Sedlec is a macabre item, the bones from some 40,000 burials in a vaulted ossuary.

THE BASICS

www.kutnahora.cz
Distance: 70km (43 miles)
Journey Time: 1 hour 15 min by bus from Florenc bus station
🛈 Sankturinovský dům, Palackého náměstí, 284 01 Kutná Hora
☎ 327 512 378

FARTHER AFIELD

🚌 EXCURSIONS

THE BASICS

Distance: 27km (17 miles)
Journey time: Local train to Nelahozeves zastávka (50 min)

Zámek Nelahozeves
www.lobkowiczevents.cz
✉ 277 51 Nelahozeves
🕐 Tue–Sun 9–5 (guided tour)
Památník Antonín Dvořáka
www.nm.cz
✉ 27751 Nelahozeves
🕐 1st and 3rd week in month, Wed–Sun 9.30–12, 1–5; 2nd and 4th week in month, Wed–Fri 9.30–12, 1–5

NELAHOZEVES

This otherwise unpretentious village on the banks of the Vltava north of Prague has two major attractions, the birthplace of composer Antonín Dvořák, and a magnificent château. Dvořák's humble home has plenty of memorabilia (tel 315 785 099), while the castle, a splendid example of Italian-inspired Bohemian Renaissance architecture, is a treasure house (tel 315 709 121 to book a tour). A permanent exhibition entitled 'Private Space: a noble family at home,' features 12 fully furnished period rooms. The building itself, approached via a bridge across a dry moat, has three completed wings, on the courtyard, in different styles. Although the interior is now mostly visited for the collections, there are many fascinating areas, particularly the Arkádové haly (Arcade Hall) and the vaulted Rytířský sál (Knights Hall).

THE BASICS

www.pamatnik-terezin.cz
Distance: 65km (40 miles)
Journey time: Around 1 hour from Florenc bus station
🚩 Terezín–Památník (Terezín–Memorial), Principova alej 304, 411 55 Terezín
☎ 416 782 225/416 782 442

TEREZIN

In World War II, the Nazis cleared this 18th-century barrack town of its inhabitants and turned it into a ghetto for Czechoslovak and German Jews. Deceitfully portraying it as a model community, they succeeded in fooling the International Red Cross, but in reality Terezín was simply a staging post for the Final Solution, and most of those incarcerated here met their end in Auschwitz. The Muzeum Ghetta (Ghetto Museum) tells the place's awful story. Outside the walls is the Malá pevnost (Small Fortress), originally an Austrian political prison, then a far more horrible jail for Gestapo victims of many nationalities.

Like all major cities, Prague has a range of accommodation, from sleek, modern hotels and magnificent converted old buildings to hostels and cottages.

Introduction

Prague offers an extraordinary range of places to stay in almost every category, with a distinct emphasis on hotels in historic buildings.

New hotels

A building boom has created an impressive increase in the number of four- and five-star establishments. Nevertheless, official room rates remain high, though you should always check for special offers. Prague is an all-seasons city, and it is prudent to book well in advance, at any time of the year.

Practical considerations

The location of your accommodation is crucial. Efficient public transport may get you quickly from your suburban hotel to the city, but since Prague is such a delight to explore on foot, you may want to look for lodgings in one of the historic quarters within walking distance of some of the main attractions. Room rates are often quoted in euros as well as Czech crowns. Credit cards are widely accepted.

Longer stays

If your stay is more than a few days, it could be well worthwhile renting an apartment or even a room in a private flat. Some of the former are in outstanding settings, with, for example, river views, while private rooms tend to be out in the suburbs.

ACCOMMODATION ADVICE

One of the most reliable kiosks at the main station is that of the Prague Information Service (P.I.S), who also can arrange accommodation at their other information offices. P.I.S also offer online reservations through their accommodation agency Pragotur ✉ Arbesovo náměstí 4, Prague 5 ☎ 221 714 130; e-mail: pragotur@pis.cz.

An excellent private apartment service is 'Apartments in Prague' ✉ Petřinská 4, Prague 5 ☎ 251 512 502; www.apartments-in-prague.org.

You can stay in grand old buildings when you visit Prague

Budget Hotels

PRICES

Between 1,850Kč and 3,000Kč per night for a budget hotel.

ATLANTIC
www.hotel-atlantic.cz
Refurbished accommodation near the Municipal House in a medium size establishment, which is a member of the Small Charming Hotels group.
🔲 H6 ✉ Na Poříčí 9, eastern New Town ☎ 224 811 084 🚇 Náměstí Republiky

BÍLÝ LEV
A good-value, 27-room place in the scruffy eastern suburb of Žižkov.
🔲 Off map J7
✉ Cimburkova 20 ☎ 222 780 430; fax 222 780 465
🚋 Trams 5, 9, 26 to Husinecká

KAFKA
Good-value, 50-room hotel on the wrong side of the tracks in Žižkov, but only 10 minutes' walk from the main train station.
🔲 G4 ✉ Cimburkova 24 ☎ 222 781 333 🚋 Tram 5, 9, 26 to Husinecká

LUNÍK
www.hotel-lunik-cz
Special offers can bring this comfortable, family-style small hotel into the affordable category. It's just a few steps from the nearest metro station and an easy walk to the top of Wenceslas Square.
🔲 H9 ✉ Londýnská 50, Vinohrady ☎ 224 253 974 🚇 Náměstí Míru

MARKÉTA
www.europehotels.cz
Bright, cheery 26-room hotel in a quiet street in the pleasant suburbs to the west of the Castle.
🔲 Off map A7 ✉ Na Petynce 45, Břevnov ☎ 220 518 316 🚇 Hradčanská, then bus 108, 174 to Kajetánka

SALVATOR
www.salvator.cz
Friendly, 32-room courtyard hotel, very near the Municipal House.
🔲 H6 ✉ Truhlářská 10, Nové Město ☎ 222 312 234 🚇 Náměstí Republiky

TARA
www.pensiontara.net
Straightforward accommodation in a tiny eight-room pension that overlooks the Havelská

HOSTELS

A number of hostels stand ready to look after the swarms of backpackers passing through Prague on their travels. A popular one offering single rooms as well as dorms and with several branches in the city and elsewhere is:
Traveller's Hostel
www.travellers.cz
🔲 G6 ✉ Dlouhá 33, Old Town ☎ 224 826 662 🚇 Náměstí Republiky

street market in the heart of the Old Town. Rooms are on the third and fourth floors and that there is no elevator.
🔲 F7 ✉ Havelská 15, Staré Město ☎ 224 228 083 🚇 Můstek

TOSCA
www.hotel-tosca.cz
Modestly furnished but comfortable accommodation just around the corner from a metro station and within walking distance of Wenceslas Square.
🔲 J10 ✉ Blanická 10, Vinohrady ☎ 221 506 111 🚇 Náměstí Míru

TŘÍSKA
www.hotel-triska.cz
A friendly place on the main drag through Vinohrady. Each of the individually furnished rooms has a refrigerator. No credit cards.
🔲 Off map J9
✉ Vinohradská 105
☎ 222 727 313 🚇 Jiřiho z Poděbrad

U ŠUTERŮ
www.usuteru.cz
Ten-room establishment in an historic building in a side street just a few steps from Wenceslas Square. Astonishing value for such a location plus a characterful restaurant on the ground floor.
🔲 G8 ✉ Palackého 4, New Town ☎ 224 948 235 🚇 Můstek

Mid-Range Hotels

AMETYST
www.hotelametyst.cz
A fresh and inviting 84-room, family-owned hotel, the equal in luxury to most of the big names and only 10 minutes' walk from Wenceslas Square.
J10 Jana Masaryka 11, Vinohrady 222 921 946 Náměstí Míru

ANNA
www.hotelanna.cz
A reliable 22-room hotel in the pleasant inner suburb of Vinohrady, less than 15 minutes' stroll from Wenceslas Square.
Off map J10
Budečská 17, Vinohrady 222 513 111 Náměstí Míru

BETLEM CLUB
www.betlemclub.cz
A small 22-room hotel offering accommodation in the same square as Jan Hus's historic Bethlehem Chapel.
F8 Betlémské náměstí 9, Staré Město 222 221 574 Národní třída

CENTRAL
www.orfea.cz
Somewhat sparse but quite adequate, the Central is located behind the Municipal House, with 68 rooms.
G7 Rybná 8, Staré

Město 224 812 041 Náměstí Republiky

CLOISTER INN
www.cloister-inn.com
Adequate 75-room hotel between the National Theatre and the Bethlehem Chapel.
F8 Konviktská 14, Staré Město 224 211 020 Národní třída

HAŠTAL
www.hastal.com
A simple 24-room hotel, in a former brewery. Nice views over a quiet square.
G6 Haštalská 16, Staré Město 222 314 335 Tram 5, 14, 26 to Dlouhá třída

HOTEL ARBES-MEPRO
www.hotelarbes.cz
Family-run hotel midway between Malá Strana and the Anděl shopping area. Ask for a quieter room overlooking the courtyard.
D9 Viktora Huga 3,

BOTELS

An alternative to conventional hotels are the 'botels' moored at various points along the banks of the Vltava. However, being rather cramped, they are less romantic than they might sound. Close to the Palacký Bridge (Palackého most) on the Smíchov quayside, try the Admirál (257 321 302).

Smíchov 257 210 410 Anděl

HOTEL 16 U SV KATEŘINY
www.hotel16.cz
Excellent-value family hotel, with 14 rooms. Close to the Dvořák Museum and the botanical gardens, and 15 minutes' walk from Wenceslas Square.
G10 Kateřinská 16, Nové Město 224 920 636 I P Pavlova

IBIS
www.accorhotels.com
The Accor group has four hotels in Prague bearing the Ibis name, all of which offer reliable, accommodation and facilities. Of the four, the most centrally located is the Ibis Praha Old Town; the claimed location is a bit of an exaggeration since it is actually in the eastern part of the New Town, albeit literally just a few steps from the Municipal House.
H7 (Ibis Praha Old Town) Na Poříčí 7, eastern New Town 221 800 800 Náměstí Republiky

MAXIMILIAN
www.maximilianhotel.com
This 1904 building has been beautifully reconstructed in art nouveau style with attention to every detail. Top of the range—try for deals.
G6 Haštalská 14, Staré Město 225 303 118 Tram 5, 14 to Dlouhá třída

MÖVENPICK

www.moevenpick-prague.com

High standard of comfort and facilities in the Smíchov branch of this chain, whose buildings are spectacularly linked by funicular. With 442 rooms.

🔢 C11 ✉ Mozartova 1 ☎ 257 151 111 🚇 Anděl

NOVOMĚSTSKÝ HOTEL

www.novomestskyhotel.cz

A small hotel on a quiet street by the New Town Hall, with a high standard for the lowish room rates.

🔢 G9 ✉ Řeznická 4, Nové Město ☎ 221 419 911 🚇 Karlovo náměstí

SAX

www.sax.cz

This 22-room hotel just off Nerudova Street offers views of Malá Strana. Now stunningly fitted out in 1960s-style retro furnishings.

🔢 C7 ✉ Janský vršek 3 ☎ 257 531 268 🚊 Tram 12, 22, 23 to Malostranské náměstí then an uphill walk

SIEBER

www.sieber.cz

This gracious family-run establishment offers 20 luxurious rooms and suites. A giant step up from the average mid-range hotel.

🔢 Off map J9 ✉ Slezská 55, Vinohrady ☎ 224 250 025 🚇 Jiřího z Poděbrad 🚊 Tram 10, 16 to Perunova

TCHAIKOVSKY

www.hoteltchaikovsky.com

A tasteful 19-room hotel near Karlovo náměstí, the Dvořák museum and the botanical gardens.

🔢 G10 ✉ Ke Karlovu 19, Nové Město ☎ 224 912 121 🚇 Karlovo náměstí/ I P Pavlova

U KRÁLE JIŘÍHO

www.hotelkinggeorge.cz

A small hotel just off the Royal Way with 17 comfortable rooms and the dubious bonus of a music club on the ground floor.

🔢 F7 ✉ Liliová 10, Staré Město ☎ 221 466 100 🚇 Staroměstská

U KRÁLE KARLA

Nestling at the foot of

COUNTRY COTTAGE

In days gone by, many of the houses on the outskirts of the city were built of timber in log cabin style. The only one remaining is U Raka (the 'House at the sign of the Crayfish'), in the tranquil surroundings of Nový Svět in the Castle quarter. It has been turned into an exquisite and expensive little hotel, beautifully fitted out in rustic style, with just a few bedrooms. www.romantikhotel-uraka.cz.

🔢 B6 ✉ Černínská 10, Hradčany ☎ 220 511 100 🚊 Tram 22, 23 to Brusnice

---

steps leading up to Hradčany Square, the comfortable King Charles exudes historic atmosphere, unsurprisingly, since the building it occupies goes back to the Middle Ages. Note that it's an uphill walk from the tram stop.

🔢 C7 ✉ Nerudova-úvoz 4, Hradčany ☎ 257 532 869 🚊 Tram to Malostranské náměstí

U LILIE

www.pensionulilie.cz

This 18-room pension is in a medieval house close to Charles Bridge. Rooms are plain, but clean and quiet.

🔢 F7 ✉ Liliová 15, Staré Město ☎ 222 220 432 🚇 Staroměstská

U MEDVÍDKŮ

www.umedvidku.cz

The 33-room pension features beautiful beamed ceilings. The famous pub of the same name is downstairs. Can get discount for cash.

🔢 F8 ✉ Na Perštýně 7, Staré Město ☎ 224 211 916 🚇 Národní třída

UNION

www.hotelunion.cz

A 57-room art nouveau hotel with comfortable and stylish rooms set in a quiet square. Well outside the city hub to the south.

🔢 G12 ✉ Ostrčilovo náměstí 4, Nusle ☎ 261 214 812 🚊 Tram 18, 24 to Ostrčilovo náměstí

Luxury Hotels

PRICES

Expect to pay upwards of 5,200Kč per night for a luxury hotel.

ADRIA

www.adria.cz

This is a stunningly restored 89-room hotel set amid the bustle of Wenceslas Square.
🔹 G8 ✉ Václavské náměstí 26 ☎ 221 081 111 ⓠ Můstek

ARIA

www.aria.cz

An exquisite and very original 52-room hotel, designed and run on the theme of music. The roof top terrace is lovely.
🔹 D7 ✉ Tržiště 9, Malá Strana ☎ 225 334 111 🚋 Tram 12, 20, 22, 23 to Malostranské náměstí

BOSCOLO CARLO IV

www.boscolohotels.com

This magnificent neo-classical palace on a square between the main station and the Municipal House is now one of Prague's most sumptuous hotels.
🔹 H7 ✉ Senovážné náměstí 13 ☎ 224 593 111 ⓠ Hlavní nadráží/Náměstí Republiky

FOUR SEASONS HOTEL PRAGUE

www.fourseasons.com/prague

Supremely luxurious conversion of a group of historic buildings near Charles Bridge. The restaurant has Prague's first Michelin star.

🔹 F7 ✉ Veleslavínova 2a, Staré Město ☎ 221 427 000 ⓠ Staroměstská

INTERCONTINENTAL

www.icprague.com

This 372-room hotel is near Josefov, and has every comfort, as well as large public rooms furnished with antiques.
🔹 F6 ✉ Náměstí Curieových 5 ☎ 296 631 111 ⓠ Staroměstská

IRON GATE HOTEL & SUITES

www.irongate.cz

Luxury in a beautifully adapted 14th-century courtyard building in a cobbled street near Old Town Square.
🔹 F7 ✉ Michalská 19, Old Town ☎ 225 777 777 ⓠ Staroměstská/Můstek

JOSEF

www.hoteljosef.com

This design hotel features 109 rooms of cool

OFFERS

The number of visitors to Prague has tended to stabilize, while provision of luxury accommodation has expanded rapidly. The rack rates charged by luxury hotels are as high as anywhere in the world, but most will offer substantial discounts at slack periods. It's worth checking whether such offers are available while planning your trip.

luxury and every conceivable amenity. Two rooms have wheelchair access.
🔹 G6 ✉ Rybná 20, Staré Město ☎ 221 700 111 ⓠ Náměstí Republiky

K&K CENTRAL

www.kkhotels.com

The equal in terms of opulent art nouveau architecture to the famous Evropa, the Central easily outclasses its rival in its comfort, convenience and inventive adaptation.
🔹 H7 ✉ Hybernská 10, Nové Město ☎ 225 022 000 ⓠ Náměstí Republiky

MANDARIN ORIENTAL

www.mandarinoriental.com

This luxury hotel is a conversion of a 14th-century monastery in Malá Strana. In an adjoining, equally venerable building, is the Spa, with a whole range of tempting treatments.
🔹 D7 ✉ Nebovidská 1, Malá Strana ☎ 233 088 888 ⓠ Tram 12, 20, 22, 23 to Hellichova

YASMIN

www.hotel-yasmin.cz

A significant addition to Prague's range of designer hotels, Yasmin upstages most of its rivals in sheer verve and trendiness. There's a Summer Garden and a Noodle Café and Bar.
🔹 H7 ✉ Politických vězňů 12, Nove Město ☎ 234 100 100 ⓠ Muzeum/Můstek

Use this section to help you plan your visit to Prague. We have suggested the best ways to get around the city and useful information for when you are there.

Need to Know

Planning Ahead

When to Go

The best times to visit are in spring, when the fruit trees of Petřín Hill are in blossom, and in early summer, before the throngs of tourists arrive. Most tourists visit between May and September. Christmas and New Year see the main squares become decorated markets and later rowdy New Year's Eve party sites.

		TIME
		Prague is one hour ahead of the UK, six hours ahead of New York and nine hours ahead of Los Angeles.

AVERAGE DAILY MAXIMUM TEMPERATURES

JAN	FEB	MAR	APR	MAY	JUN	JUL	AUG	SEP	OCT	NOV	DEC
30°F	32°F	39°F	48°F	57°F	63°F	66°F	64°F	57°F	48°F	39°F	32°F
-1°C	0°C	4°C	9°C	14°C	17°C	19°C	18°C	14°C	9°C	4°C	0°C

Spring (March–May) starts out cold and damp but turns beautiful in April and May, with blooming trees and gardens throughout the city.

Summer (June–August) can be oppressively hot and humid, with heavy rainfall.

Autumn (September–November) is a lovely time, with bright, sunny days through October and dwindling numbers of tourists. The weather has cooled considerably by November.

Winter (December–February) can be depressingly grey and cold, with the occasional heavy snowfall to brighten the mood.

WHAT'S ON

April/May *Agharta Prague Jazz Festival*: Going strong since 1992, this festival (www.agharta.cz) brings in jazz and blues acts from all over the world. It is sponsored by the Agharta jazz club (▷ 40) and is held in venues throughout the city.

May *Prague Spring Music Festival* (mid-May to early June): This international event (www.festival.cz) consists of an array of classical music concerts held in churches, palaces and halls throughout the city. It starts with a

procession from Smetana's grave in the National Cemetery in Vyšehrad, where he was buried in 1884, to the great hall named after him in the restored Obecní dům (Municipal House), where a rousing performance of his orchestral tone poem *Má Vlast* (My Country) is given.

June *Dance Prague*: International dance festival with events at various venues (www.tanecpraha.cz).

July/August Summer festivals of early music (www.tynska.cuni.cz).

December *St. Nicholas* (5 December): A multitude of St. Nicks roam the streets, accompanied by an angel who rewards good children with candy and a devil who chastizes appropriately.

Christmas Eve (24 December): Live carp are sold for the traditional Czech Christmas Eve dinner.

New Year's Eve (31 December): There are formal Sylvester balls and, outside, crowds welcome the arrival of the New Year on the streets.

NEED TO KNOW PLANNING AHEAD

Prague Online

www.prague-info.cz
Information on museums, monuments, cultural schedules and Prague history, along with tips, accommodation and general tourist listings from Prague's official tourist information service.

www.czechtourism.com
Czech Tourism's website provides information on agrotourism, UNESCO-graded monuments, cycling, mountaineering and other outdoor activities, along with useful practical planning information.

www.praha.eu.
Official web portal of the city of Prague. Overview of local events and a decent selection of tourist information.

www.radio.cz
News, history, interesting features and information on upcoming events from Radio Prague.

www.expats.cz
Leading expat bulletin board with job listings, tips on living in Prague and interesting articles.

www.praguemonitor.com
Online English-language 'newspaper' is a good source of news on current events and cultural activities.

www.praguepost.com
The online version of the city's weekly English-language paper, with news, comprehensive listings, and some visitor information.

www.prague.tv
City guide with accommodation finder, expat gossip and survival tips.

USEFUL TRAVEL SITE

www.fodors.com
A complete travel-planning site. You can research prices and weather; book air tickets, cars and rooms; pose questions to fellow travellers; and find links to other sites.

INTERNET CAFÉS

Planeta
One of the city's best-value internet cafés.
⊞ H5 ✉ Vinohradská 102, Vinohrady ☎ 267 311 182; www.planeta.cz
⏰ 0.40–0.60Kč per minute
Ⓜ Jiřího z Poděbřad

The Globe
Coffee, food and books. Plug-ins for laptops.
⊞ E5 ✉ Pštrossova 6, Nové Město ☎ 224 934 203; www.globebookstore.cz ⏰ 1.5Kč per minute Ⓜ Národní třída

Kava Kava Kava
Pleasant café with good coffee. Free Wi-Fi with a purchase. Also has computers downstairs for surfing.
⊞ D–E5 ✉ Národní 37 (in the Plat´yz courtyard), Staré Město ☎ 224 228 862; www.kava-coffee.cz
J2Kč per minute
Ⓜ Národní t´řída

Getting There

ENTRY REQUIREMENTS

Tourists from the UK, Canada, US and most European countries do not need visas.
Be sure to check the latest requirements before visiting as they can change at short notice.

DRIVING

● Road regulations are much the same in the Czech Republic as in the rest of Europe. The alcohol limit for drivers is zero and spot checks are frequent.
● Speed limits in built-up areas (indicated by place-name signs) are 50kph (31mph). Outside built-up areas the limit is 90kph (56mph) and on motorways it is 130kph (80mph).
● A vignette (sticker) permitting the use of motorways must be purchased and displayed. Buy them at post offices or large petrol stations. Rental cars should already have them.
● Headlights must be on between November and March.
● Trams must be given priority.
● First-aid kit, warning triangle and spare light bulbs must be carried.

AIRPORTS

Ruzyně Airport is 17km (10 miles) northwest of downtown Prague and is served by direct flights from most major European cities, as well as New York and Atlanta. There are shops, bars and restaurants. The national airline is ČSA (head office: ✉ V Celníci 5, Nové Město ☎ 239 007 007).

ARRIVING BY AIR

Airport information ☎ 220 113 314 (www.prg.aero). The most straightforward link from Ruzyně Airport to downtown is by minibus to Náměstí Republiky, on the eastern edge of the Old Town. The bus runs every half hour 5.30am–9.30pm. Pay at the Cedaz desk in the arrivals hall and pick up the white minibus in front of the terminal. The trip takes 20–30 minutes and costs Kč90 each way, bags included. City bus 119 goes to Dejvická metro station, from where it is only a few stops to downtown. Pick it up at the bus stand in front of the airport. Buy a Kč26 ticket inside at the DPP (Prague Transit Authority) office or from yellow ticket machines at the bus stop (change required). Buses run 5am—midnight (journey time 20 min). Bus 100 runs to Zličín metro station, which may be more convenient for western areas.

Taxis can be picked up at the airport, but agree on the approximate fare beforehand. The cost is around Kč600–Kč700 and the journey takes 25–45 minutes.

ARRIVING BY BUS

Express buses link Prague with international destinations, including London. The main coach terminal is at Florenc, on the eastern edge of downtown, where there is also a metro station. You can buy tickets at the coach terminal in Florenc but it is easier to use a travel agent.

ARRIVING BY CAR

Good main roads link Prague to all adjoining countries, and the city is now linked by motorway D5/E50 to the German autobahn network via Plzeň and the Bavarian border. The D8/E55 motorway toward Dresden and Berlin is almost complete. Prague is 1,100km (683 miles) from Calais (France), with its ferry services to Dover (UK) as well as the Channel Tunnel Shuttle. Once in Prague a car is likely to be more of a hindrance than a help.

ARRIVING BY TRAIN

Express trains connect Prague to all adjoining countries. The most convenient rail route from London is by Eurostar to Brussels, then German railways overnight trains via Frankfurt or Berlin. Most trains terminate at Hlavní nádraží (Main Station ➕ F4), though many stop (or terminate) at Holešovice in the northern suburbs or at Smíchov in the southern suburbs, both of which have good metro connections. Czech Railways (ČD) has information offices in Main Station at the north end of level 3 (domestic) and the south end of the lower hall (international) ☎ 221 111 122 (www.vlak.cz).

Getting Around

1 January, Easter Monday, 1 May (Labour Day), 8 May (Liberation Day), 5 July (SS Cyril and Methodius), 6 July (Jan Hus's Day), 28 September (St. Wenceslas's Day), 28 October (Independence Day), 17 November (Day of Students), 24–26 December.

TELEPHONES

● With the exception of emergency numbers, taxi dispatchers and the like, only 9-digit numbers are valid. If in doubt, call directory inquiries ☎ 1180.

● Most public phones now take phone cards, on sale in kiosks and post offices.
Telephoning from your hotel may cost four times the standard rate.

● To call the Czech Republic from the UK, dial 00 420. To call the UK from Prague, dial 00 44, then drop the first zero from the area code.

● To call the Czech Republic from the US, dial 011 420. To call the US from Prague, dial 001.

PUBLIC TRANSPORT

● Public transport maps are available from the information offices at the airport and metro stations Muzeum, Můstek, Anděl, Černý Most and Nádraží Holešovice.
● Expect crowding during the rush hours (generally 7am–10am, 3pm–6pm). The young and fit should give up their seats to passengers who need them more.
● Valid for all forms of transport, tickets cost Kč18 (short trips) or Kč26 (valid 1–1.5 hours) and allow as many changes as necessary. They must be validated in the machines provided before your journey. One, three and five-day passes are available.

BUS

● Kept out of downtown to minimize pollution, buses serve all the suburban areas that the trams do not reach.

FUNICULAR

● The *lanovka* (funicular railway) climbs to the top of Petřin Hill from its Újezd station in Malá Strana via a halfway station at Nebozízek.
● You can use the normal Kč26 public transport ticket or the one, three or five-day pass.

METRO

● This showpiece system, with its fast and frequent trains and clean stations, consists of three lines: A (coded green), B (yellow) and C (red). They converge from the suburbs onto downtown, where there are several interchange stations.
● To get on the right train, check the line (A, B or C) and note the name of the terminus station at the end of the line in the direction you wish to travel; this station appears on the overhead direction signs.
● Outlying stations are relatively far apart and are intended to feed commuters to connecting trams and buses.
● Particularly useful stations are Můstek (for

Wenceslas Square and Old Town Square), Staroměstská (for Old Town Square) and Malostranská (for Malá Strana and for trams 22 and 23). Hradčanská station is 15 minutes' walk from Prague Castle.

TAXI

● Prague taxi drivers have a reputation for overcharging.

● Agree on the approximate fare before-hand. Ask for a receipt to reduce excessive demands.

● You may receive a more reliable service if you phone for a taxi or flag down a moving taxi rather than going to a taxi rank in a tourist area, where drivers have the worst reputation.

● For taxis, telephone AAA Radiotaxi ☎ 222 333 222 or Profitaxi ☎ 844 700 800.

● Smart hotels have their own taxi service, reliable but expensive.

TRAM

● The tramway system operates in close conjunction with the metro.

● The name of every tram stop appears on the stop sign and on the route map.

● Tram routes are numbered, and the tram has a destination board. Timetables are posted on the stop and are almost always adhered to.

● There is a skeleton service of night trams, with its own system of particular numbers and schedules.

● A particularly useful and scenic line is the No. 22/23, which runs from the city hub (at Národní třída) right through Malá Strana, past Malostranská metro station, then climbs to the back of Prague Castle (Pražský hrad stop) and continues to Strahov Monastery (Pohořelec stop).

● On weekends between April and November an old-timer tram (Route No. 91) trundles along the tracks. It's a fun way of seeing the city.

MONEY

● There are plenty of cash machines in Prague, including at the airport, and instructions are usual-ly in English as well as Czech.

● Children, students and older people are entitled to discounts for many servic-es and attractions, though you might need to prove eligibility (passport or student card).

VISITORS WITH DISABILITIES

Many of the things that make Prague an enchant-ing city—cobblestoned streets Gothic towers with breathtaking views and red trams—can be notori-ously difficult for visitors with disabilities to negoti-ate. The metro, too, has limited access; check which stations have facili-ties first. The website of the local organization Pražská organizace vozíčkářů (POV) has com-prehensive lists (in Czech) of accessible buildings (www.pov.cz).

Essential Facts

MONEY

The Czech crown (*koruna česká* or Kč) is divided into 100 virtually worthless hellers (*halé ř*). There are coins for 50 hellers, and for 1, 2, 5, 10, 20 and 50 crowns, and notes in denominations of 50, 100, 200, 500, 1,000, 2,000 and 5,000 crowns.

50 Koruna

100 Koruna

200 Koruna

1000 Koruna

CUSTOMS REGULATIONS

● The guidelines for EU residents (for personal use) are 800 cigarettes, 200 cigars, 1kg tobacco; 10 litres of spirits (over 22 percent), 20 litres of aperitifs, 90 litres of wine (60 can be sparkling wine), 110 litres of beer.
● The limits for non-EU visitors are 200 cigarettes or 100 cigars or 250g tobacco; 2 litres of wine; 1 litre of spirits; and personal items totalling 6,000Kč in value.
● Antiques and 'rare cultural objects' require an official certificate from a recognized museum or art gallery (which the dealer may already have obtained) when being exported from the Czech Republic.

ELECTRICITY

● 220 volts, 50 cycles AC, fed through standard Continental two-pin plugs.

ETIQUETTE

● Czech manners tend to be formal. Titles such as Doctor must not be ignored, and hands should be shaken when offered.
● Dress is less formal than it was. Neat casual wear is acceptable in most restaurants and tourist theatres. Smart dress is expected in other theatres and at the opera.
● Diners share tables in busy eateries and exchange greetings: *dobrý den* (good day) and *dobrou chuť* (enjoy your meal).
● Czechs invariably say *dobrý den* (hello) and *na shledanou* (goodbye) when entering or leaving an establishment.
● If you are invited to a Czech home, take flowers or a gift and remove your shoes at the door.

MONEY MATTERS

● There are bureaux de change, but banks and ATMs often give better exchange rates.
● Credit cards are in increasing use.

OPENING HOURS

● Banks: Mon–Fri 8–5.

● Shops: many downtown shops stay open until late weekdays and are also open weekends. In the suburbs and elsewhere, shops are open Mon–Fri 9–6, Sat 9–1.

● Museums and galleries: Tue–Sun 9/10–5. Most close Mon, except the National Museum and Prague Castle (open daily); the Jewish Museum is open Sun–Fri. Some museums also close for lunch.

PLACES OF WORSHIP
● Roman Catholic: sv Tomáše (St. Thomas's Church) ⊠ Josefská 8, Malá Strana Ⓜ Malostranská Ⓔ English Mass Sun 11am
● Anglican: sv Klimenta (St. Clement's Church) ⊠ Klimentská, Nové Město Ⓜ Náměstí Republiky Ⓔ English-language service Sun 11am
● Jewish: Staronová synagóga (Old/New Synagogue, ▷ 26–27) ⊠ Pařížská and Červená Ⓜ Staroměstská Ⓔ Services Mon–Thu 8am, Fri sunset, Sat 9am

STUDENT VISITORS
● Few discounts are available for students, but keeping out of the most popular tourist spots makes Prague an affordable city.
● All aspects of youth travel are dealt with by the Student Agency ⊠ Ječná 37/39, Nové Město ☎ 224 999 666 Ⓜ I P Pavlova

TOILETS
● 'WC', 'muži/páni' (Men) and 'ženy/dámy' (Women) are useful signs to remember.
● Public facilities are rare; look in restaurants, cafés, metro stations, etc.
● Public toilets often require a fee of Kč5/7.

LOST PROPERTY

The office is at ⊠ Karoliny Světlé 5, Staré Město ☎ 224 235 085

MEDICAL TREATMENT

Visitors from EU countries, including Britain, are entitled to free emergency medical treatment, though a charge may be made for medicines. Make sure you have your blue European Health Insurance Card with you. Private medical insurance is necessary for citizens of other countries, and is still advised for EU citizens. Your hotel reception will help direct you to appropriate treatment facilities. Hospitals and clinics used to dealing with foreigners include:

Nemocnice Na Homolce (public hospital)
✚ Off map A9
⊠ Roentgenova 2
☎ 257 271 111
Ⓜ Bus 167 from Anděl Metro station to last stop

Canadian Medical Care (private clinic)
✚ Off map A4
⊠ Veleslavínská 1
☎ 235 360 133
Ⓜ Tram 20, 26 to Nádraží Veleslavín

Language

Czech is a Slavic language, particularly closely related to Slovak and Polish, less so to Russian and the South Slav languages. Like them it has a complex grammar and many inflections. Pronunciation can be a problem for foreigners, but one bonus is that the language, unlike English, is pronounced as it is written, invariably with the stress on the first syllable of the word. Most Czechs dealing with visitors from abroad will speak at least some English, but it is always worthwhile learning a few stock phrases and becoming familiar with signs.

SHOPPING

Can you assist me please? *Pomůžete mi, prosím?*

I'm looking for... *Hledám...*

Where can I buy...? *Kde dostanu...?*

How much is this/that? *Kolik stojí tohle/tamto?*

When does the shop open/close?
Kdy tady otevíráte/zavíráte?

I'm just looking, thank you.
Děkují, jenom si prohlížím.

I'll take this. *Vezmu si to.*

Do you have anything less expensive/
smaller/larger?
Máte něco levnějšího/menšího/většího?

Are the instructions included?
Jsou u toho pokyny pro uživatele?

Do you have a bag for this?
Máte na to tašku?

I'd like a kilo of... *Prosím kilo...*

This is the right size. *To je správná velikost.*

Do you have this in...? *Máte to v...?*

Is there a market? *Je tady někde trh/tržnic?*

USEFUL WORDS

yes *ano*
no *ne*
please *prosím*
thank you *děkuji*
you're welcome
prosím/nemáte zač
excuse me! *Promiňte!*
where *kde*
here *tady*
there *tam*
when *kdy*
now *teď?*
later *později*
why *proč*
who *kdo*
may I/can I? *můžu?*

MONEY

Is there a bank/currency exchange office near-by? *Je tady někde blízko banka/směnárna?*

I'd like to change sterling/dollars into crowns (Kč, Czech currency)
Anglické libry/americké dolary za české koruny (Kč) prosím...

Can I use my credit card to withdraw cash?
Mohu vybírat hotovost na svoji kreditní kartu?

GETTING AROUND

Where is the train/bus station?
Kde je tady vlakové/autobusové nádraží?

Does this train/bus go to...?
Jede ten vlak/autobus do...?

Does this train/bus stop at...?
Staví ten vlak/autobus v...?

Please stop at the next stop.
Zastavte mi na další zastávce, prosím.

Where are we? *Kde jsme?*

Do I have to get off here? *Musím tady vystoupit?*

Where can I buy a ticket?
Kde si mohu koupit lístek?

Is this seat taken? *Je tady obsazeno?*

Where can I reserve a seat?
Kde si mohu rezervovat místo?

Please can I have a single/return ticket to...
Prosím jízdenku/zpáteční jízdenku do...

Where is the timetable? *Kde je jízdní řád?*

GENERAL QUERIES

Where is the tourist information office/desk, please?
Kde je informač středisko pro turisty, prosím?

Do you have a city map?
Máte mapu města?

Can you give me some information about...?
Promiň informace o...?

What is the admission price?
Kolik stojí vstupné?

Are there guided tours?
Máte obhlídku s průvodcem?

Can we make reserva-tions here?

Můžeme si tady rezervo-vat?
How much is a ticket?
Kolík stojí lístek?

Where do they go?
Kam to jezdí?

DAYS OF THE WEEK

Monday *pondělí*
Tuesday *úterý*
Wednesday *středa*
Thursday *čtvrtek*
Friday *pátek*
Saturday *sobota*
Sunday *neděle*

NEED TO KNOW LANGUAGE

Timeline

WHITE MOUNTAIN

In 1620 the Protestant army was routed at the Battle of White Mountain. Protestant leaders were executed in Old Town Square and Czechs who refused to reconvert to Catholicism emigrated en masse. A largely foreign nobility loyal to the Habsburgs, was installed, and Prague was beautified with churches and palaces. The court made Vienna its main seat and Prague became a sleepy provincial town.

FIRST REPUBLIC

Established in 1918, the First Czechoslovak Republic was a model democracy in many ways. However, it suffered from the insoluble problem of a large German minority.

From left: Jerome de Prague, burned as a heretic; Cathedral of St. Vitus; Jan Palach burned himself to death in political protest; John Lennon Wall; crosses representing executed noblemen; radical preacher Jan Hus

7th or 8th century AD Prague's legendary foundation by Princess Libuše.

10th century Trading settlements are set up in Lesser Town and Old Town.

1231 King Wenceslas I fortifies the Old Town with 13 towers, walls and a moat.

1253–78 Reign of King Otakar II, who extends and fortifies Lesser Town, inviting German merchants to settle there.

1415 Radical preacher Jan Hus is burned at the stake.

1576–1611 Reign of eccentric Emperor Rudolph II.

1620 Battle of White Mountain.

1848 Austrian General Windischgrätz puts down a revolt led by students, but Czech nationalism continues to grow.

1914–18 Czechs are dragged against their will into World War I on the Austrian side. Many soldiers desert or join the Czechoslovak Legion fighting for the Allies.

1938 Czechoslovakia is forced to give up the Sudetenland to Nazi Germany.

1939 Prague is occupied by Nazi Germany and not liberated until 1945.

1945–47 Expulsion of the 3 million German minority from Czechoslovakia.

1948 Communists, the most powerful party in the democratically elected goverment, stage a coup d'état. As a result Stalinist repression follows.

1968 Prague Spring (▷ side panel).

1977 Dissident intellectuals sign Charter 77, a call for the government to apply the Helsinki Agreements of 1975. Many are harrassed and imprisoned.

1989 The Velvet Revolution. Václav Havel is chosen as president.

1993 Czechoslovakia splits into the independent states of Slovakia and the Czech Republic.

1999 The Czech Republic joins NATO.

2002 Catastrophic floods wreak havoc in Prague and throughout the country.

2003 Havel is replaced as president by former prime minister Václav Klaus.

2004 The Czech Republic joins the European Union.

2008 Klaus is narrowly re-elected to a second five-year term.

PRAGUE SPRING

In the 'Prague Spring' of 1968, Czechoslovakia's Communist party, under Alexander Dubček, promised to create 'Socialism with a human face'. Terrified at this prospect, the Soviet Union sent in tanks and took the government off to Moscow in chains. The last Soviet troops left in 1991.

PROTEKTORAT

In 1939, German troops marched into Prague, and Czechoslovakia became the 'Protectorate' of Bohemia-Moravia. Nazi rule was brutal, spectacularly so after the assassination of Reichsprotekor Heydrich, while the Holocaust brought to an end 1,000 years of Jewish history in the Czech lands. In May 1945, after the longest Nazi occupation in any European country, the people of Prague liberated their city and welcomed in the Red Army.

NEED TO KNOW TIMELINE

Index

Prague's
25 Best

WRITTEN BY Michael Ivory
UPDATED BY Mark Baker
DESIGN WORK Jacqueline Bailey
COVER DESIGN Tigist Getachew
INDEXER Marie Lorimer
IMAGE RETOUCHING AND REPRO Michael Moody and Sarah Montgomery
EDITOR Apostrophe S Ltd
REVIEWING EDITOR Linda Cabasin
SERIES EDITOR Marie-Claire Jefferies

© AA Media Limited 2009 (registered office: Fanum House, Basing View, Basingstoke, Hampshire RG21 4EA, registered number 06112600).

ISBN 978-1-4000-0382-2

SEVENTH EDITION

IMPORTANT TIP
Time inevitably brings changes, so always confirm prices, travel facts, and other perishable information when it matters. Although Fodor's cannot accept responsibility for errors, you can use this guide in the confidence that we have taken every care to ensure its accuracy.

SPECIAL SALES
This book is available for special discounts for bulk purchases for sales promotions or premiums. Special editions, including personalized covers, excerpts of existing books, and corporate imprints, can be created in large quantities for special needs. For more information, write to Special Markets/Premium Sales, 1745 Broadway, MD 6–2, New York, NY 10019 or email specialmarkets@randomhouse.com.

Colour separation by Keenes, Andover, UK
Printed and bound by Leo Paper Products, China
10 9 8 7 6 5 4 3 2 1

A03803
Maps in this title produced from mapping © MAIRDUMONT / Falk Verlag 2009
Transport map © Communicarta Ltd, UK

The Automobile Association would like to thank the following photographers, companies and picture libraries for their assistance in the preparation of this book.

Abbreviations for the picture credits are as follows – (t) top; (b) bottom; (c) centre; (l) left; (r) right; (AA) AA World Travel Library.

1 AA/C Sawyer; 2/3t AA/C Sawyer; 4/5t AA/ S McBride; 4 AA/J Wyand; 5 AA/S McBride; 6/7t AA/S McBride; 6cl AA/C Sawyer; 6cc AA/J Wyand; 6cr AA/S McBride; 6bl AA/C Sawyer; 6bc AA/J Smith; 6br AA/S McBride; 7cl AA/T Souter; 7ccl AA/J Smith; 7ccr AA/S McBride; 7cr AA/C Sawyer; 7bl AA/C Sawyer; 7bcl AA/C Sawyer; 7bcr AA/J Smith; 7br AA/S McBride; 8/9t AA/ S McBride; 10/11t AA/S McBride; 10tr AA/J Smith; 10ctr AA/J Smith; 10/1c AA/J Wyand; 10/1b AA/C Sawyer; 11tl AA/ S McBride; 11cl AA/J Smith; 12/13t AA/ S McBride; 13tl Digitalvision; 13ctl AA/J Smith; 13c AA/J Wyand; 13cbl AA/J Wyand; 13bl AA/J Wyand; 14/5t AA/ S McBride; 14tr AA/J Smith; 14cr AA/J Wyand; 14bcr AA/J Smith; 14br AA/J Smith; 16/7t AA/ S McBride; 16t AA/J Smith; 16tc AA/J Smith; 16bc AA/ S McBride; 16b AA/J Smith; 17t AA/J Smith; 17tc AA/J Wyand; 17bc Image 100; 17b AA/J Smith; 18t AA/ S McBride; 18tc AA/J Wyand; 18c AA/C Sawyer; 18cb AA/J Smith; 18b AA/C Sawyer; 19(I) AA/J Wyand; 19(II) AA/J Smith; 19(III) AA/J Wyand; 19(IV) AA/C Sawyer; 19(V) AA/C Sawyer; 20/1 AA/J Wyand; 24l AA/J Smith; 24/5 AA/J Smith; 25r AA/J Smith; 26l AA/J Smith; 26tr AA/J Smith; 26br AA/J Smith/Jewish Museum, Prague; 26/7b; AA/J Smith; 27tl AA/ J Smith; 27bl AA/ J Smith; 27r AA/ J Smith; 28l AA/J Wyand; 28/9t AA/J Wyand; 28/9b AA/S McBride; 29t AA/J Wyand; 29bl AA/C Sawyer; 29br AA/S McBride; 30l By Alphonse Mucha/Mucha Trust/BAL, AA/S McBride; 30c AA/ S McBride; 30r By Alphonse Mucha/Mucha Trust/BAL, AA/S McBride; 31 AA/J Smith; 32l AA/J Smith; 32/3tr AA/J Wyand; 32br AA/C Sawyer; 33t AA/C Sawyer; 33bl AA/S McBride; 33br AA/J Smith; 34l AA/J Smith; 34c AA/J Smith; 34r AA/J Smith; 35t AA/J Wyand; 35bl AA/J Smith; 35r AA/J Smith; 36t AA/J Wyand; 36bl AA/S McBride; 36br AA/J Wyand; 37 AA/J Smith; 38 AA/J Smith; 39 AA/J Smith; 40t AA/J Wyand; 41 AA/J Smith; 42t AA/S McBride; 42b AA/J Wyand; 43 AA/J Wyand; 46l By Alphonse Mucha/Mucha Trust/BAL, AA/J Smith; 46r AA/S McBride; 47l AA/C Sawyer; 47r AA/J Smith; 48l AA/J Wyand; 48r AA/J Wyand; 49l AA/S McBride; 49r AA/J Smith; 50 AA/J Smith; 50/1t AA/J Smith; 50/1b AA/J Smith; 51t AA/J Smith; 51bl AA/J Smith; 51br AA/S McBride; 52 AA/C Sawyer; 52/3t AA/J Smith; 52/3b AA/C Sawyer; 53 AA/J Wyand; 54t AA/J Wyand; 54bl AA/J Smith; 54br AA/J Wyand; 55t AA/J Wyand; 55bl AA/J Wyand; 55br AA/J Smith; 56 AA/J Smith; 57 AA/J Smith; 58 Photodisc; 59 Photodisc; 60t Digitalvision; 60b AA/J Smith; 61 AA/J Smith; 62 AA/T Harris; 63 AA/J Smith; 66 AA/J Wyand; 671 AA/C Sawyer; 67r AA/J Wyand; 68 By Alphonse Mucha/Mucha Trust/BAL, AA/ J Wyand; 68/9t AA/J Wyand; 68br AA/ J Wyand; 69t AA/C Sawyer; 68/9b AA/S McBride; 69br AA/C Sawyer; 70l AA/S McBride; 70c AA/S McBride; 70r AA/S McBride; 71l AA/J Smith; 71r AA/J Smith; 72 AA/J Smith; 72/3t AA/C Sawyer; 72/3b AA/S McBride; 73t AA/S McBride; 73bl AA/S McBride; 73br AA/S McBride; 74l AA/J Wyand; 74/5 AA/S McBride; 75 AA/S McBride; 76t AA/J Wyand; 76bl AA/J Smith; 76br AA/C Sawyer; 77t AA/J Wyand; 77bl AA/T Souter; 77br AA/J Smith; 78 AA/J Smith; 79t AA/J Smith; 79b AA/J Smith; 80 AA/T Souter; 81 AA/T Souter; 84 AA/J Wyand; 84/5t AA/S McBride; 84/5b AA/T Souter; 85 AA/ J Wyand; 86l AA/J Smith; 86c AA/J Smith; 86r AA/S McBride; 87l AA/J Smith; 87r AA/J Wyand; 88l AA/C Sawyer; 88r AA/J Wyand; 89t AA/ J Wyand; 89b AA/ J Wyand; 90 AA/ J Wyand; 90bl AA/C Sawyer; 90br AA/C Sawyer; 91 AA/J Smith; 92t Photodisc; 92c Brand X Pics; 93t AA/C Sawyer; 94 AA/C Sawyer; 95 AA/C Sawyer; 98 AA/J Wyand; 98/9t AA/ J Wyand; 98/9b AA/C Sawyer; 99t AA/J Wyand; 99bl AA/C Sawyer; 99br AA/C Sawyer; 100t AA/J Smith; 100bl AA/J Smith; 100br AA/J Smith; 100/1t AA/J Smith; 101bl AA/J Smith; 101br AA/J Smith; 102l AA/ J Wyand; 102r AA/ J Wyand; 103t AA/ J Wyand ; 103l AA/J Smith; 103r AA/ J Wyand ; 104t AA/ J Wyand; 104bl AA/ J Smith; 104br AA/C Sawyer; 105t AA/ J Wyand ; 105bl AA/C Sawyer; 105bcl AA/C Sawyer; 105bcr AA/ J Wyand ; 105br AA/ J Wyand; 106t AA/ J Wyand; 106bl AA/ J Wyand; 106br AA/ J Wyand; 107 AA/ J Wyand; 108t AA/C Sawyer; 108tr AA/J Smith; 108tcr AA/J Smith; 108c AA/S McBride; 108br AA/J Smith; 109t AA/C Sawyer; 110/1t AA/C Sawyer; 112 AA/C Sawyer; 113 AA/J Smith; 114/5 AA/ J Wyand; 116/7 AA/ J Wyand; 117 AA/J Smith; 118/9t AA/J Wyand; 120/1 AA/ J Wyand; 120b MRI Bankers' Guide to Foreign Currency, Houston, USA; 121 AA/C Sawyer; 122/3t AA/J Wyand; 122c AA/ J Wyand; 124/5t AA/ J Wyand; 124bl AA; 124cb AA; 124br AA/J Wyand; 125bl AA/ J Wyand; 125bc AA/C Sawyer; 125br AA.

Every effort has been made to trace the copyright holders, and we apologise in advance for any accidental errors. We would be happy to apply the corrections in the following edition of this publication.